Connecting
For
Coherence

Connecting
For
Coherence

A
Guide to
Building Sentences
With Syntax And Logic

Dick Heaberlin

Writing Style 2

Orange House Book
San Marcos, Texas

For Additional Information Visit the Author's Website at
dickheaberlinwrites.com

ISBN 978-0-9794964-0-0

About This Book

For many years I have been using in my classes much of the material in this guidebook. This guidebook like my Writing Style 1—*English Syntax*— doesn't depend on a previous knowledge of English syntax, but those doing the exercises will probably benefit more from them if they have first completed the work in Writing Style 1. Through the explanations, examples, and exercises in this guide, I emphasize using syntax and logic to connect sentences and teach users to connect the information of their prose and thus please readers by the clarity of their writing. I introduce various grammatical concepts and ask users to construct sentences according to specific instructions and specific examples. Gradually the sentences become more complex as users move from writing with one structure to writing with that structure in compounds and series. When there is only one answer to an exercise, an answer is provided in Appendix 1.

Contents

Connecting With Syntax

Lesson 1

Connecting Agents to Actions

I have chosen to classify the base sentences of English as dynamic or stative, according to their verb. A dynamic sentence has a subject which acts. I could call this an *actor*, but that would suggest the actor on stage, so I will refer to this actor or doer as the *agent*. So the agent does something. What he does is an action, and in this dynamic kind of sentence, the action is coded into the verb. For example, in

Tim Todd swings.

Tim is the subject, and *swings* is the verb. But the information about Tim Todd, the agent, and his action could be encoded as the subject of a stative sentence if we made Tim Todd the possessor of the action as in

Tim Todd's swing

and added a comment or judgment following a *be* verb, for example,

Tim Todd's swing is awkward.

I will call this second kind of base sentence *stative* because there is no movement in the verb phrase. In this type of structure the agent has become a noun, and the agent is in the possessive form indicated by the *s* and the apostrophe.

In the first sentence, the writer reports that Tim Todd has acted, but she is not forced by her choice of structure into commenting on that action. She may wish to exercise her option to do so by including an adverbial of manner such as *awkwardly* or *with awkwardness*. But if she has begun her sentence with "Tim Todd's swing," she no longer has an option — she must make some comment or judgment in order to complete the sentence. If she does not wish to comment, she has painted herself into a corner by the way she began the sentence. But if she does, there is a good reason to use this structure. It is a way of focusing much attention on the judgment word, *awkward*.

Tim Todd's swing is awkward.

Exercise 1

Change the sentence to a possessive agent and a noun. Answers are provided in Appendix 1. Throughout this guidebook when there is only one answer to an exercise, an answer will be provided there.

1. I worked.   *Example: my work*

2. I suggested.   *Example: my suggestion*

3. I insisted.   *Example: my insistence*

4. I perused.

5. I renewed

6. I planned.

7. I stated.

8. I reverted.

9. I delayed.

10. I persevered.

11. I continued.

12. I destroyed.

13. Sally flirted.

14. Bill resigned.

15. Tom distributed.

16. Tom converted.

17. Tom sneezed

18. Carl complained.

19. Max repeated.

Exercise 2

Now reverse the procedure and change the noun phrase to a sentence.

1 my help   *I helped.*

2. my assistance

3. my accusation

4. my disapproval

5. my doubt

6. my belief

7. my desire

8. my reversal

Exercise 3

Add an adjective or noun to the action-noun phrases to create a stative sentence.

1. My swing was <u>*awkward.*</u>

2. My return was   .

3. My dive was   .

4. My refusal was   .

5. My burp was   .

6. My glance was   .

7. My distribution was   .

Stative sentences do not always have actions as subjects. And stative sentences may be converted to noun phrases to make still other stative sentences.

Exercise 4

Convert the following sentences to noun phrases by converting the adjective into a noun.

1. Mary was beautiful.   *Mary's beauty*

2. Fred was insistent.

3. Fred was angry.

4. Carol was hasty.

5. Mike was cautious.

6. Hal was undecided.

7. Mike was lazy.

8. Sally was flirtatious.

Exercise 5

Use the noun phrases in Exercise 4 and make new stative sentences.

1. Mary's beauty   Mary's beauty was extraordinary.

2.

3.

4.

5.

6.

7.

8.

So we have these two kinds of base sentences — stative and dynamic. Obviously, there are good uses for both kinds. They both are needed to allow us to communicate. I prefer the dynamic for the general everyday tasks of writing. It has great strength and flexibility. Its name is well-chosen because prose in which it is the most common structure is dynamic, flowing. The reader has no trouble in following such prose. The stative sentence may blend in well with the dynamic. But a prose in which the stative is the most common structure is often difficult to read and disconcerting to the reader

Anyone can write dynamic sentences easily by beginning them with an agent. To do so requires no special ability. But beginning writers often look at such sentences and think that they are too simple, too uncomplicated to be good. They think good sentences must be elaborate, impressive. They are wrong. But dynamic sentences can be made more elaborate, more impressive, and still be clear.

Humans are most commonly the agents of our sentences. We may refer to the human by name, Tim Todd. We may employ a personal pronoun — *he, she,* or *I* — or an indefinite pronoun — *anyone, someone,* or *no one.* Or we may use a common noun — *boy, writer,* or *hero.* And we can write sentences with other agents: *machines* run, *cars* pass, *rocks* fall, *pliers* hold, *dogs* bark, *wasps* sting. For agents, we could use insects, animals, machines, tools, even planets. But I am most interested in helping you work with sentences with human subjects because you will use them more in your everyday writing.

What can Timothy Todd do?

He can eat, drink, swallow, choke, strangle, smile, groan, belch, scream, flirt, wave, walk, run, swim, go, move, fall, jump, jive, or dance. And that's just on his day off. Sometimes he even sleeps. All of these verbs are called intransitive because there is not a noun phrase following them which answers the question *what*.

And Timothy can do things to things. He can pare an apple, cut it, core it, slice it, chop it, dice it, mince it, and bake it into a pie. These verbs that explain what actions Tim does to the things are called transitive verbs. In these, there is a noun phrase following that answers the question *what*.

If Tim cuts, etc, the apple, he has to be doing it at some time and place. We may not care when and where, so we may not report this information. But we may want the readers to know about the place and time of the action, so we tell them,

He cut the apple on the chopping block.

or

He baked a pie yesterday.

We say that *on the chopping block* and *yesterday* are modifiers of the verbs. I will call any word or phrase which modifies a verb an adverbial. I will also call a single word modifier such as *yesterday* an adverb. The phrase "on the chopping block" is adverbial. It is composed of the preposition *on* and the noun phrase *the chopping block*, which is called the object of the preposition.

Some beginning writers believe, and some teachers teach that grammatical subordination is related to importance. They insist that information in structures considered grammatically subordinate should be and will be less important than that in the structure modified. It is a nice theory. But such is not the case. Grammatical subordination has little to do with importance of the material to the reader or writer. To decide what is important in the sentence, we need to consider why we write sentences in the first place. Most of the time we write to convey to the readers information they did not previously have. Why else would they bother to read? The new information in the sentence is most important. Often the reader knows or can guess the information in the subject and verb, but the key piece of information may be in the adverbial. For example, if we read of Tim putting together a pie, we can assume he must bake it. This information needs to be included when we describe how he bakes a pie, but we are more concerned with how. If we write,

Tim baked the pie for forty-five minutes at 400 degrees.

the two adverbial prepositional phrases—*for forty-five minutes* and *at 400 degrees*—convey significantly more important information than the subject or verb. At any rate, the general rule we will work with is that importance is not related to grammatical subordination but is related closely to what is old and new information. It is also related to position. Typically the old information will come at the first of the sentence to reveal the connection of the sentence to previous sentences. And the new information will usually come at the end of the sentence and will receive greater emphasis there, simply by being there — whatever its grammatical structure.

I like adverbials for many reasons but mainly because they convey all the important little details that make life so interesting. They tell me about time, place, direction, material, method, reasons, motives, frequency, duration. Here is a group of sentences, each of which illustrates a type of adverb. Adverbials come in many grammatical forms, but for now I am restricting them to single word adverbs and prepositional phrases.

*Tim ran **off**.*	Direction
*He went **to Austin**.*	Direction
*He went **at five o'clock**.*	Time
*He went **on a bus**.*	Means
*He went **with Susan**.*	Accompaniment
*Tim made the pie **with Jonathan apples**.*	Material
*He cut them **carefully**.*	Manner
*He cut them **with care**.*	Manner
*He cut them **with a sharp knife**.*	Instrument
*Tim visited **often**.*	Frequency
*He stayed **for several days**.*	Duration
*He came **on Friday**.*	Time
*He came **for rest**.*	Reason
*He came **under certain circumstances**.*	Condition

*He lay **on the couch**.*   Place

In addition to the prepositional phrases we have studied, there are other units which function as adverbials. One of these is the noun phrase. If the noun refers to a time, it can function as an adverbial of time, duration, or frequency. Here are three examples:

*He came **Friday***   Time
*I stayed **three days**.*   Duration
*He came **every day**.*   Frequency

If the noun is *way*, then it can function as an adverbial of manner.

*He dresses **an odd way**.*

Exercise 6

Identify all adverbials by writing above them appropriate words from this list:

A. Point in Time   F. Manner
B. Frequency   G. Material
C. Duration   H. Means
D. Place   I. Accompaniment
E. Direction.   J. Reason/motive

1. Bill went to Austin.

2. Bob put the towel on the table.

3. Fred plays with care.

4. Tom works every day until five.

5. I stayed here all day because of my illness.

6. I made the biscuits with whole-wheat flour.

7. I finished the lesson at five.

8. I did the work alone.

9. He did the job a funny way.

10. He quit his job last semester.

11. He did it out of spite.

12. He works carelessly.

13. He seldom remembers mother's day.

14. Every day he goes to work drunk.

15. He walked toward the beach.

16. He made the roof of cedar.

17. He went to the store for milk.

18. He worked for money.

19. He stared at her in an angry manner.

20. They fought without rest.

21. They stayed in the barn on the floor.

22. In the beginning I was happy.

23. I began happily.

Exercise 7

Write sentences according to the directions and examples. In each sentence, begin with a pronoun, a common noun, or a proper noun for a person. Follow that with a dynamic verb.

1. Write a sentence with an adverbial of place and time.

Example: He came here yesterday.

2. Write a sentence with an adverbial of manner and of duration.
   Example: He waited patiently throughout the day.

3. Write a sentence with an adverbial of place and time.
   Example: We stopped at the ranch yesterday.

4. Write a sentence with adverbials of place and manner.
   Example: He worked at the radial arm saw carefully.

5. Write a sentence with an adverbial of direction and manner.
   Example: He dived into the water with care.

6. Write a sentence with an adverbial of material.
   Example: They worked with wood.

7. Write a sentence with an adverbial of cause.
   Example: He quit because of the low pay.

8. Write a sentence with an adverbial of means.
   Example: He came by bus.

9. Write a sentence with an adverbial of direction and time.
   Example: Bob walked along the path at five o'clock.

10. Write a sentence with an adverbial of place and motive.
    Example: He went to Austin for a party.

11. Write a sentence with an adverbial of time and condition.
    Example: He left early in case of heavy traffic.

12. Write a sentence with an adverbial of direction, accompaniment,

Lesson 2

Connecting with Compounds and Series

I wrote in the last lesson about how a writer can take base sentences and form them gradually into more complex structures. You learned that the agent could do certain things and that what he did could be expressed by the verb. And you learned that the verb could be modified and that when it is, we call the structures modifying it adverbials, and that adverbials answer such questions as when, where, why, how, how often, how long, under what circumstances, with whom, with what, and out of what. There are enough concepts here that even with these few elements we can form rather complicated base sentences, for example,

Tim Todd always goes to Austin on a motorcycle by way of Buda.

The four adverbs in the sentence make it rather complex even though it remains a base sentence. You also learned that the agents can do what they do to things — that the verbs can take objects — and that verbs with objects are called *transitive.* So in the sentence, "Tim sliced the apples," apples are what Tim did the action of slicing to. So the noun *apples* is the direct object of the verb.

Next you will learn something quite valuable to a writer — how to connect using compounds and series and how to do it well with subtlety and sophistication.

The agent can be compounded and put into series. We can say,

Tim Todd and Mike Torres are playing basketball against Fred and Bill.

or

Tim, Mike, Fred, and Bill are playing basketball.

The first has two compounds, the second a series. But series of subjects are relatively uncommon because the subject is usually the old information. The other parts of the base sentence are frequently placed in series or compounds — the verbs, the adverbs, and objects — because they often communicate several pieces of similar new information. By compounding them, we tell the reader that they are similar without having to use words to point out the similarity.

Let's return to Tim and his apple pie.

Tim Todd peeled the apple quickly with the dull vegetable peeler. Then he split it down the middle with one bold stroke of the sharp paring knife.

These sentences are again base sentences with several adverbials. They seem neither too long nor too short. Most readers would feel comfortable with them. They would think that each sentence gave them an adequate amount of new information, and they would recognize the connection between the sentences provided by the pronoun agent subject he and the adverb then. But if I, as writer, decided that the information conveyed by the adverbs was really unnecessary to my purpose or the readers' needs, I might cut the sentence down a bit. After all, most people know what you pare and slice with. I might include information about the instrument used for cutting if I used something unusual to cut with, perhaps a machete. So I leave that out. And isn't cutting down the middle what split means? And, finally, I decide that my reader doesn't need to know how quickly Tim did it or with how many strokes, so I am left with

*Tim Todd **peeled** the apple. Then, he **split** it.*

Now our reader is going to be unhappy with me. He is not getting his customary amount of new information with each sentence. The pace is too slow, so he is upset. I solve the problem by compounding — by bringing the two base sentences into a single double-verb sentence. And I get

*Tim Todd **peeled** and **split** the apple.*

or

Tim Todd peeled the apple and split it.

The original sentence, however, was not too long to be compounded. I could have said

*Tim Todd **peeled** the apple quickly with the dull vegetable peeler and then **split** it down the middle with one bold stroke of the sharp paring knife.*

Which of the several sentences I use is related to my purpose. If my subject is just pie preparation, I may consider some of the details not worth my trouble and omit them. If I want to tell about Tim's personality, I may wish to use the longer sentence which tells us something about the young man, particularly if we consider the difficulties of cutting quickly with a dull peeler and the bold stroke. Such details are often better at revealing personality than a flat statement about someone.

The difference between a compound and a series is not great. Let us return to the preparation of Tim's pie.

> *Tim Todd **peeled** the apple quickly with the dull vegetable peeler. Then he **split** it down the middle with one bold stroke of the sharp paring knife. Next he **chopped** it into small pieces with a large French chopping knife in the manner of Julia Child.*

If I leave the adverbials out of each sentence, I have three short sentences with which to dissatisfy my reader.

> *Tim Todd peeled the apple. He split it. He chopped it.*

I again bring the base sentences together, now into a triple-verb sentence.

> *Tim Todd **peeled, split**, and **chopped** the apple.*

I call this a series. But I am not limited to a triple-based sentence. The series can run to as many items as I think effective. Remember Tim's effort in the first lesson.

> *Tim can pare an apple, cut it, core it, slice it, chop it, dice it, mince it, and bake it into a pie.*

This is made up of nine base sentences. Unusual I grant. But it serves its purpose. Such long series serve to suggest rapid movement or the agent's concentration on the tasks at hand. And I do not believe any reader would find the sentence annoying, especially after it is placed in context.

So far, we have looked at compounding only single-word verbs, not verb phrases, not those with auxiliary verbs. Verb phrases work much the same as single-word verbs, but there are a few quite important differences.

> *Tim **may leave** home for Boston during September. He **may stay** with a friend for a short time. Then he **may rent** a small apartment.*

These sentences can obviously be stripped and be made into a rather conventional three part series.

> *Tim **may leave** for Boston, **stay** with a friend for a short time, and then **rent** an apartment.*

The *may* could be repeated and used before all three main verbs, but with short verb phrases such as these, the repetition is unwarranted, even intrusive.

> Tim **may leave** home for Boston, **may stay** with a friend for a short time, and then **may rent** a small apartment.

But even this may be acceptable in some situations. What if I followed the sentence with this one?

> He may do a lot of things, but nobody can guess what he will do — as wishy-washy as he is.

Now the repetition of *may* serves to emphasize a basic character trait of the agent.

Let's look at another series of sentences.

> Tim **had** finally **written** his term paper on procrastination at the last possible minute with the last page of typing paper. He **had caught** the last possible bus. Then he **had arrived** just at the moment of his teacher's departure from the school.

I can change this into a series of verbs without reducing the adverbs or repeating the auxiliary verb.

> Tim **had** finally **written** his term paper on procrastination at the last possible minute with the last page of typing paper, **caught** the last possible bus, and then **arrived** just at the moment of his teacher's departure from the school.

This is a possible variation, but I see no particular advantage of it over a series of sentences. And repeating the auxiliary verb *had* helps the reader only a little in perceiving the structure.

> Tim **had** finally **written** his term paper on procrastination at the last possible minute with the last page of typing paper, **had caught** the last possible bus, and then **had arrived** just at the moment of his teacher's departure from the school.

I prefer the first series, the series of three separate sentences. But of the several choices left to me, one is most obvious. I don't have to make a series of this material. I could make a compound verb and follow it with the final sentence.

*Tim **had** finally **written** his term paper on procrastination at the last possible minute with the last page of typing paper and **had caught** the last possible bus. He **had arrived** just at the moment of his teacher's departure from the school.*

Yet I still prefer the first one. I think I would use it, with the addition of an and to the last sentence to signal that this is the final sentence in the series. So I end with,

*Tim **had** finally **written** his term paper on procrastination at the last possible minute with the last page of typing paper. He **had caught** the last possible bus. And he **had arrived** just at the moment of his teacher's departure from the school.*

Exercise 1

Write a sentence to fit the instructions and the example.

1. Use a series of three dynamic verbs and some type of adverbial modifier for each.
    Example: He worked till midnight, partied till dawn, and slept till time for work again.

2. Write a sentence with a single dynamic verb but with a series of three prepositional phrases which use the same preposition.
    Example: He works with a skill saw, with a saw protractor, and with a nail gun.

3. Write a sentence with compound dynamic verbs. Each of the verbs will be modified by an adverb of manner with -ly.
    Example: The prodigal son left happily and returned sadly.

4. Write a sentence with a preposition that has three objects.
    Example: She had worked in a restaurant, an insurance agency, and a grocery store.

5. Write a sentence where you have two direct objects modified by the same possessive adjectival.
    Example: She lost her wallet and her car keys.

6.   Write a sentence with four direct objects modified by possessive adjectivals. *Example*: *She lost her wallet, her car keys, her books, and even her shoes.*

7.   Write a series of three action verbs, each of which has same direct object. *Example*: *They washed, rinsed, and dried the dishes.*

8.   Write a series of four dynamic verbs, each of which has at least an adverb modifier or a direct object. *Example*: *We worked for two hours, played basketball for about fifteen minutes, went to a movie, and returned home late for dinner.*

9.   Write a series of six dynamic verbs and as many adverbials and objects as you want. *Example*: *He watered the horses, slopped the pigs, weeded the garden, cleaned the barn, vaccinated the pigs, and repaired the tractor.*

10. Write a sentence with a stative verb and a compound predicate adjective. (Some stative verbs are *be, become, remain, seem*) *Example*: *He is old and grey.*

11. Write a sentence with a stative verb and series of three predicate nouns. Use a form of the verbs, *be, become,* or *remain*. *Example*: *He became a scholar in the fifth grade, an athlete in high school, and a lover in college.*

12. Write a sentence with a stative verb and series of three predicate adjectives. *Example*: *He has been happy with Mary, angry with Susan, and furious with Carla.*

13. Write a sentence with a stative verb and series of four predicate adjectives. If the series is followed by a period, you may omit the *and*. *Example*: *He is my boss, my friend, my alarm clock, my dog.*

14. Write a sentence with a predicate adjectives compounded with *but*. *Example*: *We were happy about the victory but sad about the injury to Tim.*

15. Write a sentence with an object of preposition compounded with *or*. *Example*: *She is going to the party with Tom or Harold.*

Exercise 2

Complete the series of sentences by using dynamic verbs with at least one adverbial or object.

Example:
1. *Bob James robbed the bank in Jefferson City.*
2. He *studied the layout of the bank.*
3. *He waited outside for the customers to leave.*
4. *Then he rushed in with a pistol in his hand.*

1. Bob James

2. He

3. He

4. He

Exercise 3

Write a paragraph of six sentences all of which have the same agent.

Lesson 3
Connecting with Passive Voice

The base sentence we have been writing is quite versatile. We can use it to do a variety of tasks. One variation on some forms of this base sentence is called passive voice. And the passive voice sentence is one of great importance to a writer. It may not be needed often but when it is needed, it is really needed. I will explain to you the reasons why passive is appropriate or inappropriate in given circumstances, thus giving you information which will give you confidence that you have made the right choice.

But before a writer can make a careful, conscious choice whether to use a passive sentence or not, he must be able to recognize it. Some of the base sentences we have been working with can easily be converted to the passive voice — those with direct objects.

Tim sliced the apple.

can be converted to

The apple was sliced by Tim.

and

Tim ate the pie.

can be converted to

The pie was eaten by Tim.

Notice that in each of these passive voice variations of our base sentence we have a past form of the verb *be*. The eight forms of be are *be, am, is, are, was, were, been,* and *being.*

*The apple **was** sliced by Tim.*
*The pie **was** eaten by Tim.*

Notice also that the verb is in the past-participle form, *-ed* for regular verbs and *-en* for most irregular verbs. For a sentence to be passive it must have both of these. When you are trying to decide whether a sentence is passive, you should look first at the last verb element to see if it is in the past-participle form. Then, you should look in front of that last verb to see if there is a form of the verb *be*. Here are some sentences first in the active voice form and then in the passive. Notice that all eight forms of the verb *be* are illustrated.

Active: Bill stole the watch.
*Passive: The watch **was** stolen by Bill.*

Active: Mom loves me.
*Passive: I **am** loved by mom.*

Active: Mary treats Bill fairly.
*Passive: Bill **is** treated fairly by Mary.*

Active: I polish the cars every day.
*Passive: The cars **are** polished every day by me.*

Active: The principal may punish Bill
*Passive: Bill may **be** punished by the principal.*

Active: The policeman was handing Bill a ticket.
*Passive: Bill was **being** handed a ticket by the policeman.*

Active: Bill had baked the pie.
*Passive: The pie had **been** baked by Bill.*

There is still another transformation I could make on each of these sentences should I choose — omitting the *by* prepositional phrase, thus leaving out the agent.

*The watch **was** stolen.*
*I **am** loved.*
*Bill **is** treated fairly.*
*The cars **are** polished every day.*
*Bill may **be** punished.*
*Bill was **being** handed a ticket.*
*The pie had **been** baked.*

At times leaving out this information works well, but I will warn you in great detail later of the dangers of making this change to the passive sentence.

Exercise 1

Convert the following active voice sentences to passive. Remember each must have some form of the verb *be*.

1. I finished the job.
   Example: *The job was finished by me.*

2. Tim did the work.

3. Tom may have destroyed the evidence.

4. Tom struck me.

5. Belle Starr and Jesse James committed crimes.

6. Joe was eating the chips again.

7. I have cut the lines.

8. They sank the ship.

Exercise 2

Reverse the procedure and change the following passive-voice sentences into active-voice sentences.

1. Baseballs were thrown into the stands by the batboy.

   Example: The batboy threw the baseballs into the stands.

2. Fish are often seen by scuba divers.

3. Plankton is eaten by whales.

4. Carbohydrates are stored by the body.

5. Jim Smith will be rewarded for his efforts by the boss.

6. Geometry is being offered by the junior high school during the summer term.

7. Soon passive voice will have been taught by the teacher.

I need to add to something I mentioned earlier. The subject of the sentence in most good prose is not a place of emphasis. Instead, it is used to provide a connection to previous sentences. It tells the reader that the sentence concerns something which has been mentioned previously. We might write:

Tim Todd drove into Austin late Saturday afternoon to meet Susan at Lady Bird Lake.

The sentence following this one might begin in several ways, all of which would be connected to the first in some way. Most likely it would begin with either *Tim* or *he* and continue the same focus as the first sentence. But we may wish to shift our focus. So we may choose to begin the sentence with *she* focusing on Susan, with *That afternoon*, focusing on Saturday afternoon, with *Lady Bird Lake*, focusing on the place, with *his car*, focusing on the means of transportation implied by *drive*, with *A meeting*, focusing on the meaning of the infinitive *to meet*, or with any one of several other subjects implied in the first sentence. At any rate, the second sentence will in most cases begin with something previously mentioned. So if we begin with *he*, we mean to say, "Here is more I have to say about Tim Todd, whom I mentioned in the previous sentence." And using *he* is an effective, simple, dynamic way to connect sentences, but because the agent is not new information, it is among the least important pieces of information in the sentence although it needs to be there to make the connection. We are reading the sentence to find out what more Tim did.

The point of all this is that we do not choose passive voice to emphasize the information placed in the subject position. Instead, we choose passive voice in order to connect smoothly to previous sentences and to emphasize what happened to the subject or who did the thing to the subject. For example, let us consider choosing between several forms of a base sentence.

Tim was hired.
Foleys hired Tim Todd.
Tim was hired by Foleys.

It is meaningless to discuss out of context which of these sentences is better than the other. The first might serve a writer well following such a sentence as

Tim Todd applied for a job at Foleys yesterday. (He was hired.)

The second might be suitable to follow a sentence such as

Foleys was considering hiring several young men for a management trainee position. (Foleys hired Tim Todd.)

The third might suitably follow a sentence such as

Tim Todd got a job yesterday. (He was hired by Foleys.)

In the first sentence, the key piece of new information is "What was done to Tim?" So it is appropriate that this information appear at the end in the place of greatest emphasis. We know clearly from the previous sentence who did the hiring, so there is no need to repeat it by adding it at the end. But in the last sentence "by Foleys" is the key piece of new information. Everything else in the sentence we already know." And "by Foleys" appears in the proper place of importance at the end of the sentence. Here are some guidelines we learn from these three examples.

1. When the person or thing affected is the key piece of new information, we use the active voice.

    Bill is a good hunter. He shot a tiger.

Here the information in the subject and verb of the second sentence is old since it is apparent from his being a hunter. Only the information about the tiger is new, so it belongs at the end.

2. When the action done to that person or thing is the key piece of new information, we use the passive voice without the *by* prepositional phrase.

    The tiger had been raiding the villages, but yesterday it was shot.

Here what happens to the tiger is most important, so it is presented last.

3. When the agent is the key piece of new information, we use passive voice with the *by* prepositional phrase.

    A tiger had been raiding the village, but it was shot yesterday by our friend Bill.

By placing "by our friend Bill" last, we put the new information in its proper place at the end of the sentence and thus emphasize it.

Exercise 3

Employing the guidelines above, choose which sentence might best follow this one: "Bill Simpson had been stealing welding rods from his construction job."

1. Yesterday, a policeman arrested him.
2. Yesterday, he was arrested.
3. Yesterday, he was arrested by a policeman.

Exercise 4

Write a brief explanation of how you applied the guidelines in order to make the choice.

Exercise 5

Employing the guidelines above, choose which sentence might best follow this one: "Bill complained a lot."

1. He was despised by his roommate, his boss, his teachers, his coach, his brother, even perhaps his mother.
2. His roommate, his boss, his teachers, his coach, his brother, even perhaps his mother despised him.
3. He was despised.

Exercise 6

Write an explanation of how you applied the guidelines in order to make the choice.

Exercise 7

Employing the guidelines above, choose which sentence might best follow this one: "Fred went shopping."

1. Beans, carrots, celery, asparagus, red peppers, and sweet onions—the new kind— were bought by him.
2. Beans, carrots, celery, asparagus, red peppers, and sweet onions—the new kind— were bought.

3. He bought beans, carrots, celery, asparagus, red peppers, and sweet onions—the new kind.

Exercise 8

Write an explanation of how you applied the guidelines in order to make the choice.

Lesson 4

Connecting to Verbs

I explained in Lesson 1 how a writer could easily convert the dynamic kind of base sentence into an action-noun phrase. Let's repeat the earlier exercise in order to get that concept clearly in mind.

Exercise 1

Convert the dynamic kind of base sentence into a noun phrase of action.

1. He retired.   *his retirement*

2. We evaded.

3. We discovered.

4. She deceived.

5. She pleaded.

6. Fred apologized.

Being able to make these conversions may not seem important to you at first. But it is one of the most critical skills you can develop in order to become a skillful writer or editor of prose. Let us add one complication, an adverb, to be converted into an adjective modifying the action noun.

7.   Bill swung wildly.   *Bill's wild swing*

8.   They complained loudly.   *their loud complaints*

9.   He ran for six yards.   *his six-yard run*

10. He ran a long way.   *his long run*

11. Bill smiled cunningly.

12. Bill burped loudly.

13. Sara performed magnificently as Ophelia.

14. Fred played in center field with enthusiasm.

15. Sam responded speedily.

Now let's add one more complication, a direct object, which will also be converted into the object of a preposition in a prepositional phrase which will modify the action noun.

16. He fought cancer. *his fight against cancer*

17. He discovered a cure. *his discovery of a cure*

18. He described the house.

19. He avoided Roger.

20. Carl manipulates his friends.

Now that we have practiced converting the dynamic kind of base sentences into noun phrases of action, we may consider various ways we may make use of them. We can make an action the subject of a stative sentence as we did in the first lesson. So we could form the following sentences from some of the noun phrases in Exercise 1.

His fight against cancer was unending.
His discovery of a cure for cancer was surprising.
Their loud complaints were insulting.
His long run was exciting.

But most of the time, we do not want to use this kind of sentence, preferring instead the dynamic sort of base sentence. These noun phrases of action can serve us quite well, though, as objects of preposition.

Tom quit his job because of his boss' loud complaints about Tom's poor work.

Complaints and its modifier and *work* and its modifiers are action noun objects of *because of* and *about*. This is a good, clear, well-written sentence. The reader can easily understand who did each of the actions — quitting, complaining, and performing

Using this action-noun phrase is one way we can make verbs into nominals — convert them to function as nouns do, answering the question what? We can also employ the form of the verb called the present participle — the one with an -ing ending — to serve as nouns do.

The easiest way for me to explain this is by using examples, so let us look again at Exercise 1.

1. He retired.   *his retirement*
2. They returned.   *his return*
3. We discovered.   *our discovery*
4. She deceived.   *her deception*
5. She pleaded.   *her plea*
6. Fred apologized.   *Fred's apology*

Instead of converting these to nouns, we can convert them to present participles by removing the *-ed* ending, adding the *-ing* ending and by changing the subject into a possessive form.

1. his retiring

2. their returning

3. our discovering

4. her deceiving

5. her pleading

6. Fred's apologizing.

Exercise 2

Convert these to present-participle phrases.

7.   Bill swung wildly.   *Bill's swinging wildly*

8.   They complained loudly.

9.   He ran for six yards.

10. He ran a long way.

11. Bill smiled cunningly.

12. Bill burped loudly.

13. Sara performed magnificently as Ophelia.

14. Fred played in center field with enthusiasm.

15. Sam responded speedily.

16. He fought cancer.

17. He discovered a cure.

18. He described the house.

19. He avoided Roger.

20. Carl manipulates his friends.

Connecting with Prepositions

What can present participles be used for? They can be subjects of sentences.

Bill's swinging wildly surprised me.
Bill's wild swinging caused him to fall.

But these present participles — when they are subjects — force the writer to make some comment about them. They are used more frequently and effectively as objects of prepositions.

*He finished the theme by **working all night**.*

Let us go back to the action-noun phrases we were discussing earlier and see how similar they are to present-participle phrases. An example we had then was

Tom quit his job because of his boss' loud complaints about Tom's poor work.

We could convert either action-noun phrase to a present participle. For now let us just change *complaint* to *complaining*.

*Tom quit his work because of his boss' **complaining** loudly about Tom's poor work.*

Exercise 3

Convert the base sentence into first an action-noun phrase and then a present-participle phrase and use each to replace *doing something*.

1. **Base:** He accused Tom.
He avoided suspicion by doing something.
   Example of Noun Phrase: *He avoided suspicion by his accusations against Tom.*
   Example of Present participle: *He avoided suspicion by accusing Tom.*

2. **Base:** He withdrew from the competition.
The match ended because of his doing something.

Example of Noun Phrase: *The match ended because of his withdrawal from the competition.*
Example of Present-participle Phrase: *The match ended because of his withdrawing from the competition.*

3. **Base:** He described the circumstances.
He helped the new people by doing something.
Use noun phrase:

Use present-participle phrase:

4. **Base:** Bob contemplated the nature of the universe.
Bob avoided his problems by doing something.
Use noun phrase:

Use present-participle phrase:

5. **Base:** He demonstrated his courage.
He inspired his men by doing something.
Use noun phrase:

Use present-participle phrase:

6. **Base:** He assisted with the care of his grandmother.
Frederick pleased his family by doing something.
Use noun phrase:

Use present-participle phrase:

If these phrases are so similar, how are we ever going to know which one to use? A good guideline is, "To be more formal use the action-noun phrase; to be less formal use the present participle."

These are obviously kinds of double-base sentences, ones used best with a single agent doing both actions.

Bill won the match. He putted consistently well on the back nine.

The second base has the same agent as the first, so we can omit *his* in the second.

Bill won the match by putting consistently well on the back nine.

Notice that the second base is used as the object of the preposition *by* and that the entire prepositional phrase is a modifier of the verb *won*, explaining how or why he won. So the second base is grammatically subordinate to the verb of the first base, but that does not make it less important. The information in the second base is the key piece of new information in the sentence. Notice the situation when this sentence is placed in context.

> *Bill Traughber captured the annual Flatonia Invitational Tournament yesterday. He won by putting consistently well on the back nine.*

Notice that there is no new information in the subject and verb of the second sentence. *He won* simply repeats the information in the first sentence in order to lead into the important new information at the end of the second. I could have left out the *he won* and made the new information part of the first.

> *Bill Traughber captured the annual Flatonia Invitational Tournament yesterday by putting consistently well on the back nine.*

But I chose not to, thinking that that was probably too much new information for a single sentence and that this gave too little emphasis to the importance of the victory.

Now let us look at some of the prepositions we use to introduce actions that modify actions and what logical connection the phrases they introduce have on the verb.

Prepositions	Logical Connection
because of	causation, motive
for	causation, motive
by	manner, reason
with	manner
without	manner
despite	contrast, concession, surprise
instead of	contrast, concession, surprise
in addition to	addition
in case of	condition

at the time of	time
during	time
before	time
after	time

Here are some examples:

She was sleeping in a hammock at the time of the explosion.
The bank guard was watching in case of another attempt at a robbery.
Fred left without washing any dishes.
He won in spite of committing fourteen double faults.
Cynthia wrote a thesis in addition to teaching two composition classes.
She succeeds because of her attention to detail.

Notice how easy to read these are. There is no need for any mark of punctuation because these adverbials are in their customary position at the end of the sentence, and the beginning of the structure is marked by the connecting word — the preposition.

Exercise 4

For this exercise use human subjects and dynamic verbs.

1. Write a sentence with a present-participle phrase as object of *into.*
   Example: He nagged his wife into vacationing in Southern Georgia in the summer.

2. Write a sentence with present-participle phrase as object of *without.*
   Example: He left the party without eating anything.

3. Write a sentence with present-participle phrase as object of *after.*
   Example: He destroyed the evidence after seeing the police at his door.

4. Write a sentence with present-participle phrase as object of *before.*
   Example: He resigned his commission before marrying Mary.

5. Write a sentence with present-participle phrase as object of *for*.
    Example: *The principal punished the children for throwing erasers across the room.*

Exercise 5

1. Write a sentence in which you have a compound present-participle phrase as object of *in addition to*.
    Example: *He robbed a bank in addition to holding up stages and rustling cattle.*

2. Write a sentence in which you have compound present-participle phrase as object of *by*.
    Example*: He won the game by serving well and making few unforced errors.*

3. Write a sentence in which you have a compound present-participle phrase as object of *after*.
    Example: *The ship arrived late after running through a hurricane and having emergency repairs.*

Exercise 6

Now write sentences with series of three or more present-participle phrases.
1. Use the preposition *after*.
    Example: *Fred left home after cleaning his room, washing the dishes, and taking out the trash.*

2. Use the preposition *without*.
    Example: *Tim always leaves without combing his hair, brushing his teeth, or using deodorant.*

3. Use the preposition *for*.
    Example: *Marvin was rewarded for working long hours, staying awake, and not complaining.*

Connecting with Subordinating Conjunctions

There is still another way to connect adverbial concepts to the verb. We can employ a subordinating conjunction.

*Foley's would not consider him for the job **because** he applied late.*

There are subordinating conjunctions which parallel most of the prepositions introduced in the last lesson and more.

Here are some of the single word subordinating conjunctions: after, although, as, because, before, if, once, provided, providing, since, so, supposing, that, though, unless, until, when, where, whereas, while.

Here are some of the compound subordinating conjunction: along with the fact that, as a result of the fact that, as often as, as if, as soon as, as soon as it happened that, as though, at the place that, at the time that, because of the fact that, despite the fact that, due to the fact that, during the time that, in addition to the fact that, in case, in case that, in contrast to the fact that, in hopes that, in order that, in spite of the fact that, owing to the fact that, plus the fact that, even though, every time that, in the event, in the event that, now that, provided that, providing that, since the time that, so that, supposing that, with the fact that, within the period of time that,

Exercise 7

Convert the prepositional phrase to an adverbial clause with a subordinating conjunction.

1. He quit in spite of liking the job.

   Example: He quit although he liked the job.

2. He lost the match because of his poor serves.

3. He was attending college at the time of his sister's marriage.

4. He left upon the entrance of Fred.

5. Tim cried after the fight with Mark.

6. He conceded defeat after losing the second set.

Connecting Verbs to Objects

In Lesson 4, you learned how you can convert base sentences into action nouns and present-participle phrases and then use the phrases as subjects of sentences and as objects of prepositions. For example,

Fred destroyed the sandcastle.

can be changed to

Fred's destruction of the sand castle.

and

Fred's destroying the sandcastle

or

destroying the sandcastle

and these could be used in

Fred's destroying the sand castle surprised me.
I was surprised by Fred's destroying the sand castle.

In this lesson, you will learn how these phrases and others like them made from base sentences can be embedded into matrix sentences as direct objects. These matrix sentences have verbs that are frequently followed by phrases and clauses made from base sentences. I have subdivided the matrix sentence types and base structure types into sub-groups. Now I will list them, and then you will write some sentences of all these types.

Type of Nominal Structures	Example
1. Action Nouns	*Fred's destruction of the sandcastle*
2. Present-participle Phrases	*Fred's destroying the sandcastle*
3. Infinitive Phrases	*for Fred to destroy the sandcastle*
4. Infinitive Phrases with **what** words	*what to destroy*

| 5. Clauses with **that** | *that Fred destroyed the sandcastle* |
| 6. Clauses with **what** words | *what Fred destroyed* |

Kinds of Matrix Verbs

1. Thinking/Feeling verbs
2. Informing verbs
3. Sensing/Learning verbs
4. Starting/Stopping verbs
5. Assisting/Allowing verbs
6. Causing verbs

Neither of these lists are complete, but they are sufficient for our purposes here.

Examples of the Six Kinds of Nominal Structures with a *Think* Word

Action-noun phrase

Fred remembers his destruction of the sandcastle.

Present-participle phrase

Fred remembers destroying the sandcastle.

Infinitive phrase

Fred remembered to destroy the sandcastle.

Infinitive phrase with **what** word

Fred remembered what to destroy.

That clause

Fred remembers that he destroyed the sandcastle.

What clause

Fred remembers what he destroyed.

Here are some examples of how we may use the *what* words: *who, whom, whose, which, what, why, where, when,* and *how*. I will use another **think** verb in these examples: ***know.***

*I know **what** you bought.*
*I know **which** you bought.*
*I know **who** bought the bike.*
*I know **whose** you bought.*
*I know **where** you bought it.*
*I know **when** you bought it.*
*I know **why** you bought it.*
*I know **how** you play.*
*I know **how** hard you play.*
*I know **how** you are.*
*I know **whose** bike you bought.*
*I know **which** bike you bought.*
*I know **what** bike you bought.*

Exercise 1

1. Write a sentence with a present-participle phrase following the verb *hate*.
   Example: I hate doing exercises everyday.

2. Write a sentence with a *that* clause following the verb *suspect*.
   *Example: I suspect **that** he will get here early.*

3. Write a sentence with a *where* clause following the verb *know*.
   *Example: I know **where** he works.*

4. Write a sentence with a *where*-headed infinitive phrase following the verb *remember*.
   *Example: I will remember **where** to go for the test.*

5. Write a sentence with an infinitive phrase following the verb *like* or *hate*.
   *Example: I don't like **for Hal to beat me at tennis.***

Exercise 2

1. Write a sentence with two present-participle phrases following the verb *hate* or *like*.
   Example: I like writing well and getting good grades.

2. Write a sentence with two *that* clauses following the verb *suppose*.
   *Example: I suppose **that** he arrive late and **that** he will have a poor excuse.*

3. Write a sentence with the verb *forget and* two *what* clauses.
   *Example: I forgot **when** her birthday was and **what** she wanted for a present.*

4. Write a sentence with the verb *know and* two *what*-headed infinitive phrases.
   *Example: I should know **what** to buy her and **where** to get it.*

5. Write a sentence with two infinitive phrases following the verb *like* or *hate*.
   *Example: I don't like **for Hal to beat me at tennis** or **for him to brag about it.***

Exercise 3

1. Write a sentence with a series of present-participle phrases following the verb *hate, like,* or *regret*.
   Example: I don't like mowing grass, washing dogs, or burning trash.

2. Write a sentence with a series of *that* clauses following the verb *learn*.
   *Example: I learned **that** Boston is the home of the Red Soxs, **that** they play in Fenway park, and **that** the stadium is near the home of Boston Pops.*

3. Write a sentence with a series of clauses beginning with a *what* word following the verb *forget, remember,* or *know.*

Example: I remember **what** the test covers, **where** the test will be given, and **what** I must bring.

4. Write a sentence with three infinitive phrases headed by what words following the verb *remember.*

Example: I should know **where** to go, **when** to go, and **how** to get there.

5. Write a sentence with a series of infinitive phrases following the verb *want.*

Examples: I want George **to wash** the dishes, Fred **to rinse** them, and Tom **to dry** them.

I don't want **to wash** the dishes, **to rinse** them, or **to dry** them.

I don't want **to wash, rinse,** or **dry** the dishes.

Faulty Compounds as Series

It is obviously incorrect to mix most of these constructions. In Standard English, we avoid mixing constructions in a compound or series.

*Mary hates **going** to a dance with Fred and **to see** him leave with Louise.*

There is one major exception to this rule. The *what* clauses and *what* infinitives often follow action-noun phrases in a compound or series.

*He knows the answer and **how** to get it.*
*He remembers Mary and **what** she did to him.*

Prepositions with *Think* Verbs

Verbs of thinking often take prepositions after them.

*I **think** about writing a book.*
*I **know** about living in the mountains.*

Another Kind of Matrix

We have still another way to create a matrix for the six base constructions. We can use a linking verb and an adjective of thought or feeling.

*I **am not sure** that he destroyed the sandcastle.*
*He is **sure** to destroy the sandcastle.*

And we can use the preposition *about* with these structures.

*I **am not sure about** his destruction of the sandcastle.*
*I **am not sure about** his destroying the sandcastle.*
*I **am not sure about** who destroyed the sandcastle.*
*I **am not sure about** how to destroy the sandcastle.*

Other adjectives which can be used for most of these constructions are *certain, uncertain, unsure, confident, glad, happy, angry, afraid, fearful, doubtful, scared, ashamed, resolute, determined, adamant, furious.*

Exercise 4

1. Write a sentence with a *that* clause following the adjective *confident*.
   Example: I am **confident that** I will win the next game.

2. Write a sentence with an infinitive phrase following the adjective *afraid* or *happy*.
   Example: I am **afraid that** I will not finish my essay on time.

3. Write a sentence with a clause headed by *where* following *sure about*.
   Example: I am not **sure about where** he works.

4. Write a sentence with a *where*-headed infinitive phrase following *certain about*.
   Example: I am not **certain about where** to go for the test.

5. Write a sentence with an present-participle phrase following *sure about*.
   Example: I am not **sure about** going to work today.

Matrix Embedded in Matrix

One of the most interesting things about all of this is the way a clause can be embedded into another one and that one into still another one.

We can take one of the sentences we have been working with,

I know that Fred destroyed the sandcastle.

and put

George thinks that

before it and get,

George thinks that I know that Fred destroyed the sand castle.

And then we can put

Bill is afraid that

in front of that and get

Bill is afraid that George thinks that I know that Fred destroyed the sandcastle.

Now obviously I could go on. There is no limit but good taste and judgment.

Lesson 6

Connecting with Adjectival Clauses and Phrases

I had a teacher once who told me that I should not use too many adjectives. She insisted that I use precise nouns. She wanted me to say "cowboy" rather than "a man who works cattle" and "midget" rather than "an extremely small man." And I tried to do what she wanted, but I discovered that there wasn't a name for everything I wanted to write about. And if there was a name, often I didn't know what it was. And if I knew the name of it, often my reader or listener didn't. So I discovered I couldn't get by unless I took a general noun and qualified it. I was able to get rid of those obviously redundant adjectives like those in "unmarried bachelor" and "small midget." But I thought, "Can't midgets be small and large too, for midgets?" And I thought, "What about cowboys? What if they work on a horse ranch? Are they then horseboys or maybe wranglers?" Maybe they are just ranch hands either way. Maybe I should just say, "The men who work on the horse ranch." And I'm back to an adjectival — the adjectival clause or relative clause as it is sometimes called.

Obviously, adjectival clauses are needed, particularly the first time you mention something, but they can be avoided. The first sentence below could be replaced by the second two.

> *The men who worked on the horse ranch in Wyoming during the winter thought that they were paid poorly for freezing while working so hard at repairing fences and hauling hay.*

> *The men worked on a horse ranch in Wyoming during the winter. They thought that they were paid poorly for freezing while working so hard at repairing fences and hauling hay.*

Although these sentences may be improved by further subdivision, the change makes it better.

Exercise 1

Combine into one sentence using adjectival clauses. To do this, find the common noun in the insert and replace it with one of the relative pronouns: *who, which, whom,* or *that* — whichever is appropriate. Then move the pronoun to the first of the insert if it isn't already there. Then embed the insert into the matrix following the common noun.

*Example: **Insert:** The children had tickets.*
*   **Matrix:** The children entered first.*

The children who had tickets entered first.

1. **Insert**: The man lost his job.
   Matrix: The man was unhappy.

2. **Insert:** The trees were dying fast.
   Matrix: The trees had a strange disease.

3. **Insert:** The man was arrested for forgery.
   Matrix: I know the man.

4. **Insert:** The job is dangerous and hard.
   Matrix: The man got a job.

5. **Insert:** The river was running deep.
   Matrix: Tim and Bob crossed the river.

6. **Insert**: The man was unhappy.
   Matrix: The man lost his job.

7. **Insert:** The trees had a strange disease.
   Matrix: The trees were dying fast.

8. **Insert:** I know the man.
   Matrix: The man was arrested for forgery.

9. **Insert:** The man got a job.
   Matrix: The job is dangerous and hard.

10. **Insert:** Tim and Bob crossed the river.
 Matrix: The river was running deep.

Exercise 2

Break into two sentences.
 Example: The people who were talking about Lisa's immorality were probably referring to Lisa on As the World Turns.

 Answer: The people were talking about Lisa's immorality. They were probably referring to Lisa on As the World Turns.

1. The man who watched the football practice when there was a scrimmage would leave if the team began to run pass patterns.

2. The man who talked with his buddies while he was preparing supper forgot to put baking powders in the cornbread.

3. The man who wanted to be sure to watch the final NBA playoff game went to sleep quietly on the couch shortly after the tip-off.

Now let's look at how adjectival clauses work. They begin with *who, whom, which, that, where, when, why* and *whose.* They can, of course, be compounded and placed in series, but rarely is this done well when the noun modified is the subject. Observe the problem when compounding between noun and verb,

 *The man **who** loses what he needs to do his work, **who** can't find the tools, notes, books, papers, or whatever, and **who** blames his wife for his own errors is not a fit husband.*

By the time readers get to the verb is, they may have forgotten that man was the subject of the sentence. It works much better when the series comes at the end, in the place of new information, in the place of greatest emphasis.

 *I know a foolish man **who** forgets where he put his wrenches, **who** searches fruitlessly for them for hours, and **who** then blames his wife for moving them.*

Exercise 3

1. Write a sentence with one relative clause.
   Example: *I recognized the man **who** robbed the bank.*

2. Write a sentence with two relative clause.
   Example: *I bought a car **that** gets good gas mileage and **that** is easy to repair.*

3. Write a sentence with a relative clause which begins with *where*. It must follow a noun of place.
   Example: *The room **where** I lost my wallet is locked now.*

4. Write a sentence with a relative clause which begins with *which*.
   Example: *I can write a sentence with a relative clause **which** begins with* which.

5. Write a sentence with a relative clause which begins with *when*. It must follow a noun on time.
   Example: *I remember the minute **when** we first met.*

6. Write a sentence with a series of relative clauses.
   Example: *We will award the scholarship to someone who has a 3.5 gpa, **who** lives in Hays County, and **who** is majoring in English.*

Present-participle Phrases as Adjectivals

We often identify something by what it has done.

The man who was riding in the back of the pick-up is taking chances.
The cattle which were grazing in the pasture were beautiful.

We can reduce the sentences by leaving out the *who was* and the *which were*, and then we don't have adjectival clauses to identify the nouns *man* and *cattle* but have adjectival phrases headed by present participles.

The man riding in the back of the pick-up is taking chances.
The cattle grazing in the pasture were beautiful.

Exercise 4

Convert the adjectival clause to a present-participle phrase.

*Example: The man **who was stealing** tools from his job was fired.*
*Answer: The man **stealing** tools from the job was fired.*

1. The pigeons that were roosting on the window air conditioner were cooing loudly and often.

2. I spoke to the man who was fishing from the pier.

3. The men who were playing baseball with the children were playing without gloves.

Exercise 5

1. Write a sentence with a present-participle phrase which modifies a noun.
   *Example: The people stand**ing** in line to buy tickets are getting wet.*

2. Write a sentence with two present-participle phrases which modify a noun.
   *Example: I know the people wear**ing** the silly clothes and play**ing** the kazoos.*

3. Write a sentence with a series of present-participle phrases which modify a noun.
   *Example: In the playoffs I favor the team winn**ing** the most games late in the season, play**ing** the best defense, and hav**ing** the best point guard.*

Past-participle Phrase as Adjectival

In addition to identifying a noun by something that it did, we can identify a noun by something done to it.

The bicycle which was stolen from the yard was valuable.
The bicycle stolen from the yard was valuable.

The two sentences do essentially the same thing — identify the bike by what was done to it. We derived our past participle by deleting the *who, which,* or *that,* and the past form of *be, was.*

Unless the deletion causes the sentence to be unclear, most writers prefer to use the past-participle phrase rather than the clause simply because it is shorter.

Exercise 6

Convert the adjectival clause to a past-participle phrase.

*Example: The man **who was hired** by his father was fired by his brother.*
*Answer: The man **hired** by his father was fired by his brother.*

1. The chickens that were raised in Arkansas were eaten in Texas.

2. I interviewed the man who was arrested for the crime.

3. The team which was beaten by us in the first game won the tournament.

Exercise 7

1. Write a sentence with a past-participle phrase which modifies a noun.
   Example: The food selected by the students was just junk.

2. Write a sentence with two past-participle phrases which modify a noun.
   Example: I read the books selected by the judges and given the biggest prizes.

3. Write a sentence with a series of past-participle phrases which modify a noun.
   Example: The vegetables picked, canned, and put away last spring were delicious this winter.

Lesson 7

Connecting Without Qualifying— Adjectival Structures

Participles as Nonrestrictive Modifiers

Last lesson, I explained how we use adjectival clauses, present-participle phrases, and past-participle phrases to help us tell the reader just what we are talking about, in other words to restrict the meaning of a rather general noun. I suggested that we need these adjectivals to communicate because there often just aren't any precise nouns to say what we need to say, or if there are, we or our readers may not know them. So I said we need these restricting phrases and clauses. But what if we are successful in identifying something for our readers, do we still need to modify it? We don't need to, but sometimes we may want to, want to say something — by the way or off topic — to the reader. It is a sort of an aside, a way of just sticking something in that's not particularly relevant but something the writer wants the reader to know — a kind of parenthetical expression, but not so off the topic that we feel a need to set it off in parentheses, but it is still a way of adding information that the sentence could well do without. When we use adjectival clauses as nonrestrictive modifiers, we do not introduce the clauses with *that*. Instead we use *which, who* or *whom*. Because these structures are not identifying the noun by restricting its meaning, we set them off with commas.

Exercise 1

Convert the adjectival clause to either a present or past-participle phrase.

Example: Tim Todd, who was elected cheerleader for the third consecutive year, jumped about agilely on the sidelines.

Answer: Tim Todd, elected cheerleader for the third consecutive year, jumped about agilely on the sidelines.

1. Seguin High, which was beaten three consecutive weeks, fought back by trouncing Judson 35-6.

2. My mother-in-law, who is wearing a magenta leotard, is taking low-impact aerobics.

3. Larry Bird, who was scoring with both left and right hands, led the Celtics past the Pistons.

4. Marie-Louise, who was given an award for showmanship, has retired from teaching.

5. Aunt Carol, who was stealing loquats from a neighbor's tree, was caught by policemen in five squad cars.

These nonrestrictive modifiers do not have to remain immediately after the noun to which they connect. They may be moved to the front of the sentence or to the end.

> *The little-league parents, screaming obscenities, rushed onto the field.*
> *Screaming obscenities, the parents rushed onto the field.*
> *The parents rushed onto the field, screaming obscenities.*

This structure is a very commonly used one, one particularly common in narrative writing and one often compounded and used in series.
The past-participle phrases can be moved about, too.

> *Boston, defeated by a ninth-inning Detroit rally yesterday, hopes to win with Clemons today in Cleveland.*
> *Defeated by a ninth-inning Detroit rally yesterday, Boston hopes to win with Clemons today in Cleveland.*
> *He lived on, consumed by a desire to avenge the loss of his honor.*

Exercise 2

1. Write a sentence with an nonrestrictive, end-shifted present-participle phrase.
   Example: Bob entered the room, singing some tune about dancing to a harvest moon.

2. Write a sentence with a series of nonrestrictive, end-shifted present-participle phrases.

Example: The team left the field, knowing that they had played poorly, hoping that the coach would not make them run laps, and fearing that the opposing fans would be throwing overripe fruit at them.

3. Write a sentence with a nonrestrictive, front-shifted present-participle phrase.

Realizing that there would be a quiz at the end of the class, Tim listened to the teacher

4. Write a sentence with a nonrestrictive present-participle phrase after the noun.

Example: Tim Todd, figuring he needed some gas money, began to work at the Jack in the Box in the afternoon.

5. Write a sentence with two nonrestrictive, front-shifted present-participle phrase.

Example: Taking off his coat and removing his glasses, Joe Keller leaped into the brawl

6. Write a sentence with two nonrestrictive, present-participle phrases after the noun.

Example: Louise cried, holding her handkerchief tightly against her nose and sobbing so loudly that everyone in the restaurant looked at her.

Exercise 3

1. Write a sentence with a nonrestrictive, past-participle phrase after the noun.

Example: Bob Childress, defeated in the fall election by a landslide, continued to participate actively in politics.

2. Write a sentence with a nonrestrictive, front-shifted past-participle phrase.

Example: Defeated in the semifinals by a mediocre player, Tim Todd threw his racket into the stands.

3. Write a sentence with a nonrestrictive, end-shifted past-participle phrase.

Example: Jim Cleveland went away, terrified of the gang who were extorting money from him.

Adjective Phrases As Nonrestrictive modifiers

Just as present and past-participle phrases can be derived from relative clauses, so also can adjective-headed phrases.

*Bill, **who was** happy about winning the lottery, celebrated by buying his mother a house.*

This can be shortened to an adjective phrase by dropping the *who* and *was*.

*Bill, **happy** about winning the lottery, celebrated by buying his mother a house.*

This could be further changed by shifting the adjective phrase to the front.

***Happy** about winning the lottery, Bill celebrated by buying his mother a house.*

Exercise 4

1. Write a sentence with a non-restrictive adjective phrase after the noun it modifies.

*Example: My sister, **unafraid** of the monsters which she had just read about, walked home alone*

2. Write a sentence with a nonrestrictive adjective phrase frontshifted.
*Example: **Suspicious** about the noise he kept hearing in the neighborhood and about what was making it, Marvin set up surveillance equipment.*

3. Write a sentence with a nonrestrictive adjective phrase end-shifted.
   *Example The soldier lay quietly, **tired** from their long march.*

4. Write a sentence with two nonrestrictive adjective phrases after the noun they modify.
   *Example: Billy Williams, **eager** to see what he could say about his beautiful young wife and **aware** that she would read what he wrote, wrote carefully for several hours.*

5. Write a sentence with two nonrestrictive adjective phrases front-shifted.
   *Example: **Dirty** from the blowing dust and **tired** of the noise, Michael slipped away from the crowd*

6. Write a sentence with two nonrestrictive adjectives phrase end-shifted.
   *Example: I sat there, **angry** about my friend's complaining and **sick** of all his silliness.*

Nonrestrictive Appositive Phrases

Another structure we can derive from the deletion of *who* or *which* and a *be* verb is the appositive.

*Tim Johnson, **who is** a relief pitcher for Seattle, has been selected for the all-star team.*
*Tim Johnson, a relief **pitcher** for Seattle, has been selected for the all-star team.*

We can use an appositive, modified and unmodified, for a number of useful tasks. They are seldom used in conversation but often are in writing. They are particularly good for emphasis.

*I have a job, an excellent **position** with Foley's.*
*He married a good woman, a better **wife** than he deserved.*
*Hunter wore a mask at Halloween, a gorilla **mask**.*

You can even use more than one appositive to the same noun.

*He wrote a **book,** a **book** about love and hate, a **book** about his home in East Texas.*

Obviously, these are rather showy and should not be used so often that the reader begins to be bothered by them.

Exercise 5

1. Write a sentence with an appositive to *dog.*
    Example: Tom has a hunting dog, a fearful, incompetent brute.

2. Write a sentence with an appositive to *room.*
    Example: Will walked into his room, a dirty place where only the bravest would dare go.

3. Write a sentence with an appositive to *story.*
    Example: Faulkner wrote a strange story, a tale about a bear and a boy.

4. Write a sentence with an appositive to some person.
    Example: Tricia Wilson, my neighbor, tries to find out what is happening behind every door.

4. Write a sentence with two appositives to a person.
    Example: Tricia Wilson, my neighbor and former friend, tries to find out what is happening behind every door.

Repeating other parts of speech for emphasis or amplification is much like using an appositive.

*He stood **straight, straight**er than his father.*
*He was **standing** tall, **standing** with his chest high.*
*Zachary ate **enthusiastically,** even more **enthusiastically** than his brother, Oliver.*
*She has a **hard** job, **hard**er even than leading a dance team.*
*He wanted **more** pie, **more, more, more** — always **more.***
*He went **deep** into the wilderness, **deep**er than his father, even **deep**er*

*than Boon Hoganbeck, **deep**er than was safe for one so young, so inex-perienced.*

William Faulkner didn't write the last example, but it is like many sentences he did write, for he loved these amplifications. They work well for expressing emotion. I like them, too. But I have to watch myself, or I get carried away, far away, into overly elaborate prose, prose too much like Faulkner, my hero, a worthy hero, a master of prose, one I will be imitating—if I am not careful.

Nominative Absolute

Another parenthetical construction is called a nominative absolute and is much like a very loose appositive, seeming to connect somehow to what's happening. Let's look at some examples.

*He came in, **his teeth** chattering from the cold.*
*He stood there, **his hands** raised high above his head.*
*He batted, **his back elbow** low, too low probably.*
*They arrived, **their furniture** on the car top, piled high.*
*He smiled, **his lips** drawn back weirdly.*
*We left, **the sun** low and orange on the horizon.*

Exercise 6

1. Write a sentence with the noun of the nominative absolute modified by a present participle.
   Example: He prepared to write, his right hand holding a sharpened pencil.

2. Write a sentence with the noun of the nominative absolute modified by a past participle.
   Example: He prepared to write, a sharpened pencil poised above the pad.

3. Write a sentence with the noun of the nominative absolute modified by prepositional phrase of location.
   Example: He prepared to write, a sharpened pencil in his right hand.

4. Write a sentence with the noun of the nominative absolute modified by an adjective.

Example: The dog looked terrible, his hair muddy.

To be a little more conversational, we can replace the comma with the preposition *with* and get a rather special kind of adverbial prepositional phrase of manner.

> *He came in **with his teeth** chattering from the cold.*
> *He waved **with his hands** raised high above his head.*
> *He batted **with his back elbow** low, too low probably.*
> *They arrived **with their furniture** on the car top, piled high.*
> *He smiled **with his lips** drawn back weirdly.*
> *We left **with the sun** low and orange on the horizon.*

Adverbials

Still another kind of parenthetical structure is a word or phrase—usually placed at the first—which makes some kind of comment such as how honest the writer is or what way the material should be taken, for example

> ***Honestly,*** *he escaped last night.*
> ***Ethically speaking,*** *America's the pits.*
> ***Weatherwise,*** *it's going to be a good day.*
> ***Certainly,*** *he will come.*

There are still other kinds of parenthetical expressions, but if you master these you will be well along in your progress toward a mature, flexible style.

Connecting
With Logic

Lesson 8

Connecting Actions with Time

When I took persuasive speaking in college, my professor talked about three kinds of persuasion — emotional, ethical, and logical. At the time, I thought of logical as being what he talked about — facts and data to support my arguments. We did learn about the differences between inductive and deductive reason, and he talked some about logical fallacies. But it was not until I started teaching writing that I realized the importance of logic in everyday life. The sentences we speak or write are connected through logic to some others we spoke or wrote or to the context of our speaking. We take an action or condition and connect it to another by saying that there is a relationship of time, cause, contrast, condition, location, or addition.

In the first seven lessons, we looked at connection between parts of the sentence, connections such as those between subjects and verbs, between verbs and objects, between verbs and adverbials, between nouns and adjectivals. Now we are going to use that information and talk in more detail about some of the logical concepts mentioned in some of the earlier lessons. We will look at the common means of connecting to show various kinds of logic.

Time is prevalent in our language, for we cannot write or speak a sentence without marking the verb with time. As we learned in Lesson 1, we often add information about time to the verb by using an adverbial. These could provide information about point in time or about duration.

*Bob left at three **in the afternoon.***	*Point in time*
*Bob came **yesterday**.*	*Point in time*
*Bob stayed **for three hours**.*	*Duration*
*Bob stayed **from two until three***.	*Duration*

Sometimes writers or speakers mistakenly and redundantly provide an adverbial or adverbials when the tense of the verb conveys all the writer wishes to say. One computer site I read to get the price of natural gas, sometimes redundantly says, "At this point in time the information is currently unavailable."

Connecting by Juxtaposition

We may suggest a time connection between two actions just by placing them side by side.

I walked into the classrooms. My students quit reading, closed their textbooks, and got out their notebooks.

There are no adverbials in these two sentences, but the reader knows that at the time I came in the students were reading. They then did the three actions one after the other.

Exercise 1

1. Write two sentences which have actions that occur one after the other. Do not use a connective word.
   Example: I washed the dishes. Andrea put them away.

2. Write two sentences which have actions that occur simultaneously. Do not use a connective word.
   Example: I listened to the radio. The announcer was talking about Iraq.

3. Write three sentences which have actions that occur one after the other. Do not use a connective word.
   Example: I washed the dishes. Jim rinsed them. Andrea put them away.

4. Write three sentences which have actions that occur simultaneously. Do not use a connective word.
   Example: We all worked. Bob did the dishes. Sue washed clothes. Tom took out the trash.

5. Write one sentence which has two actions that occur one after the other. Use the coordinating conjunction *and*.
   Example: I washed the dishes and put them away.

6. Write one sentence which has two actions that occur simultaneously. Use *and*.
   Example: I held the nail and hit it with the hammer.

7. Write one sentence which has three actions that occur one after the other. Use two *ands* and no comma.
   Example: I washed the dishes and rinsed them and put them away.

8. Write one sentence which has three actions that occur simultaneously. Do not use a connective word.
   Example: I petted the dog, talked to Emily, listened to the radio.

Connecting with Conjunctive Adverbs

There are several structure words we have to show a time connection between two actions or conditions. One of the most common is the conjunctive adverb. It may be rather formal, for example consider how noticeable the connectives are in these sentences.

*He completed his work. **Subsequently**, he napped.*
*He completed his work. **Afterwards**, he napped.*
*He listened to the music. **Simultaneously**, he tapped his fingers on the table.*

Given the subject matter here, I doubt that any of us would use such ponderous, formal connectives. Instead, we could mute the information while still making it available. With other more formal subjects these connectives might be quite appropriate.

*He completed his work. **Then**, he napped.*
*He napped. **Earlier**, he completed his work.*
*He completed his work. **Later**, he napped.*
*He listened to the music. **Meanwhile**, he tapped his fingers on the table.*

Sometimes people use entire prepositional phrases to replace the conjunctive adverb.

*He completed his work. **After that**, he napped.*
*He listened to the music. **At the same time**, he tapped his fingers on the table.*

Exercise 2

Use a conjunctive adverb or prepositional phrase in each of the exercises below. Choose from conjunctive adverbs such as *then, afterwards, later, earlier, meanwhile, concurrently, subsequently,* or *simultaneously*. Or use a prepositional phrase such as *within the hour, at this time, from this time, after this, since then, since that time,* or *after that day.*

1. Write two sentences which have actions that occur one after the other.
   *Example: I washed the dishes. **Later**, Andrea put them away.*

2. Write two sentences which have actions that occur simultaneously.
   *Example: I did my homework. **At the same time**, I was listening to the radio.*

3. Write three sentences which have actions that occur one after the other.
   *Example: I washed the dishes. **Then**, I rinsed them. **Later**, Andrea put them away.*

Connecting with Prepositions

I am not particularly fond of conjunctive adverbials or those prepositional phrases as the connective to show time relationships. One useful replacement connective is just the preposition itself. It is usually more informal, thus allowing more emphasis to be placed on the action of napping or on completing the work.

> *__After__ the completion of his work, Bob napped.*
> *__After__ completing his work, Bob napped.*
> *Bob napped __after__ the completion of his work.*
> *Bob napped __after__ completing his work.*
> *__Before__ his nap, Bob completed his work.*
> *__Before__ napping, Bob completed his work.*

For showing simultaneous action, I like to use the preposition *during*.

> *__During__ out meeting, we discussed the need for more teachers.*
> *We discussed the need for more teachers __during__ out meeting.*

Exercise 3

Use a preposition of time in each of the exercises below. Choose from prepositions such as *after, before, since,* or *until.*

1. Write a sentence with a prepositional phrase of action. The time of the prepositional action should be before or after the *that* of the main clause.
   Example: *Bob napped **after** completing his work.*
   ***Before** his nap, Bob completed his work.*

2. Write a sentence with a prepositional phrase of action. The time of the prepositional action should be at the same time as that of the main clause.
   *Examples: **During** out meeting we discussed the need for more teachers.*
   *We discussed the need for more teachers **during** out meeting.*

3. Write a sentence which has compound objects of prepositions with actions that occur one after the other.
   *Example: **After** washing and rinsing the dishes, Andrea put them away.*

Connecting with Subordinating Conjunctions

Instead of those effective preposition, I more commonly use the equally effective subordinating conjunction. For simultaneous action, I use *while* or *as.*

> ***While** he listened to the music, he tapped his fingers on the table.*
> ***As** he listened to the music, he tapped his fingers on the table.*
> *He tapped his fingers on the table **while** he listened to the music.*
> *He tapped his fingers on the table **as** he listened to the music.*

With *while*, we have the option of dropping out the subject and creating an elliptical expression if the subjects of both clauses are the same.

> ***While** listening to the music, he tapped his fingers on the table.*
> *He tapped his fingers on the table **while** listening to the music.*

If the subjects of both clauses are not the same and we drop the subject of the *while* clause, we commit the error called faulty ellipsis.

> **While** *listening to the music, his fingers were tapping on the table.*
> *His fingers were tapping on the table* **while** *listening to the music.*

These can be corrected in either of two ways. The poorer choice is probably to put in the omitted information.

> **While** *he was listening to the music, his fingers were tapping on the table.*
> *His fingers were tapping on the table* **while** *he was listening to the music.*

It usually works better to keep the ellipsis and put the omitted subject into the subject position in the main clause.

> **While** *listening to the music, he tapped his fingers on the table.*
> *He tapped his fingers on the table* **while** *listening to the music.*

Some compound subordinating conjunctions work well to show the time connection between two actions. Two that I use frequently are now that and as soon as.

> *As soon as I get home from work, I change into my gardening clothes.*
> *I change into my gardening clothes* **as soon as** *I get home from work.*
> *I can clear the brush more effectively* **now that** *I own a Stihl chainsaw.*
> **Now that** *I own a Stihl chainsaw, I can clear the brush more effectivel*

But I suggest that writers should avoid any compound which includes "the time that."

> **During the time that** *he was here, he was sleeping.*
> **At the same time that** *he was sleeping, I was working.*

These can be replaced by the more economical *while*.

Exercise 4

Use a subordinating conjunction of time in each of the exercises below. Choose from subordinating conjunctions such as *after, before, since, until, as soon as, now that, as, while.*

1. Write two sentences which have actions that occur one after the other.
   Example: **After** *I washed the dishes, Andrea put them away.*
   Andrea put the dishes away **after** *I washed them.*

2. Write one sentence with a subordinating clause which occurs simultaneously with the main clause.
   Example: **As** *he listened to the music, he tapped his fingers on the table.*
   He tapped his fingers on the table **while** *he listened to the music.*

3. Write a sentence with compound subordinating clauses, both of which occur at the same time as the main clause.
   Example: **While** *Bob was doing the dishes and* **while** *Sue was washing clothes, Tom was taking out the trash.*

4. Write a sentence with compound subordinating clauses, both of which occur before the action of the main clause.
   Example: **After** *Bob washed the dishes and* **after** *Sue washed clothes, I vacuumed the house.*

5. Write a sentence with a series of subordinating clauses, all of which occur after the action of the main clause.
   Example: *I washed the dishes* **before** *Sue washed clothes,* **before** *Tim vacuumed, and* **before** *Joe took out the trash.*

Connecting with Present and Past Participles

Still another way to show a time connection is by using the nonrestrictive adjectivals which we studied in a previous lesson. We can use present and past participles to show a time connection with the action of the main clause.

Here are nonrestrictive adjectival clauses turned into present and past-participle phrases by deleting the *who* and *was.*

Bill Johnson, **who was** *skydiving for the first time, was probably saying his prayers.*
Bill Johnson, **who was** *chosen head cheerleader, works hard to make the group better.*
Bill Johnson, **skydiving** *for the first time, was probably saying his prayers.*
Bill Johnson, **chosen** *head cheerleader, works hard to make the group better.*

We could leave the participle phrases here or move them to the front.

Skydiving *for the first time, Bill Johnson was probably saying his prayers.*
Chosen *head cheerleader, Bill Johnson works hard to make the group better.*

Some participle phrases work well after the verb phrase.

Bill worked hard, **planning, meeting, practicing—doing** *anything necessary to make his group better.*
Bill left the tennis court, **defeated** *by a rank beginner, someone he knew he could beat.*

Exercise 5.

1   Write a sentence with a present-participle phrase after the noun it modifies.
Example: Andrea, **sitting** *at the table, is watching Julia eat.*

2. Write a sentence with a present-participle phrase front-shifted before the subject.
Example: **Sitting** *at the table, Andrea is charting music for her choreography.*

3. Write a sentence with a present-participle phrase end-shifted.
Example: I stood there, **watching** *the parade go by.*

4. Write a sentence with a compound present-participle phrase after the noun it modifies.
Example: Andrea, **doing** *her hair and* **thinking** *about what to wear, is getting ready for the party.*

5. Write a sentence with a compound present-participle phrase front-shifted.
Example: **Running** *two miles every day and* **lifting** *weights every other day, George stayed with his routine.*

6. Write a sentence with a compound present-participle phrase end-shifted.
  *Example: I stood there, **watching** the parade go by and **wishing** that I was in it.*

7. Write a sentence with a series of present-participle phrases end-shifted.
  *Example: I spoke, **holding** my notes in my left hand, **keeping** track of the time, and **trying** to make eye contact with the audience.*

Exercise 6

1. Write a sentence with a past-participle phrase after the noun it modifies.
  *Example: Bob Johnson, **taken** out after facing only one batter, threw his glove into the dugout.*

2. Write a sentence with a past-participle phrase front-shifted.
  *Example: **Taken** out after facing only one batter, Bob Johnson threw his glove into the dugout.*

3. Write a sentence with a past-participle phrase end-shifted.
  *Example: We left the field, **defeated** again by an inferior opponent.*

4. Write a sentence with a compound past-participle phrase end-shifted.
  *Example: We left the field, **defeated** by an inferior opponent and **criticized** by our coach.*

Adjective Phrases

Similarly, we can get a nonrestrictive adjective phrase and move it around. There will be no time marker in the phrase, but the condition described in the adjective phrase exists at the same time as that of the main clause. Notice the following transformations. I take out the *who was* of the relative clause, and I am left with an adjective phrase which I can then move to the front of the sentence.

*Bill Johnson, **who was** seasick during most of the cruise, stayed in his room and saw nothing.*

*Bill Johnson, **seasick** during most of the cruise, stayed in his room and saw nothing.*

Seasick during most of the cruise, Bill Johnson stayed in his room and saw nothing.

Putting the adjective phrase at the end and combining it with past and present participles, we might get something like this:

*Bill Johnson lay in his bunk, **seasick**, **disgusted**, **thinking** that he would die.*

I usually prefer these constructions to be at the end like this rather than at the first or in the middle where, if they are long, they may cause difficulty in understanding the sentence:

Angry about not knowing where his children were even though it was past midnight and on a cold stormy night, Jim fretted.

The reader could easily get tired of waiting to find out who was angry and who was knowing.

These constructions can also cause trouble if they are excessively long after the subject:

Jim, angry about not knowing where his children were even though it was past midnight and on a cold stormy night, called his wife at work.

The reader would grow impatient waiting for the verb phrase and might even forget who the subject was.

Exercise 7.

1 Write a sentence with an adjective phrase after the noun it modifies.
   *Example: Tom Smith, **careful** about his writing, checked his essay to be sure that everything connected.*

2. Write a sentence with an adjective phrase front-shifted.
   *Example: **Sure** that the punctuation was correct, Tom Smith turned in the essay.*

3. Write a sentence with an adjective phrase end-shifted.
   *Example: I turned it in, **confident** that I had written a good essay.*

4. Write a sentence with a compound present-participle phrase after the noun it modifies.

*Example: Sue, **tired** of cooking and **sick** of eating at home, decided to go out to eat.*

5. Write a sentence with an adjective phrase, a present-participle phrase, and past-participle phrase end-shifted.

*Example: We played, **angry** about our coach's criticism, **remembering** our last defeat, **determined** to get revenge.*

Connecting with Absolute Constructions

Absolute constructions are also called Nominative Absolutes. Its action or condition is simultaneously with the main clause. It is made up of a noun in the same context as the main clause and of a modifier of that noun.

He stood there, his hands full of stolen property. — *hands* is modified by an adjective phrase

He stood there, his hands on his hips. — *hands* is modified by a prepositional phrase of location

He stood there, his hands stuck in his pockets. — *hands* is modified by a past-participle phrase.

He stood there, his teeth chattering from the cold. — *hands* is modified by a present-participle phrase.

Exercise 8.

1 Write a sentence with an absolute construction which has the noun modified by a present-participle phrase.

Example: He shaped the clay, his hands moving steadily.

2. Write a sentence with an absolute construction which has the noun modified by a past-participle phrase.

Example: He shot the ball, his wrist relaxed.

3. Write a sentence with an absolute construction which has the noun modified by a prepositional phrase of location.
   Example: He drove, the telephone in his left hand.

4. Write a sentence with an absolute construction which has the noun modified by an adjective or adjective phrase.
   Example: Macbeth stood there, his hands bloody.

Connecting with Nouns of Time

One effective and flexible way to show time relations between two actions or conditions is by using nouns of time. Sometimes they act much like conjunctive adverbs.

> *We crossed the river with the herd. The next day, we pushed on toward Dodge City.*

They can be a lot like prepositions.

> *The day after the river crossing, we pushed on toward Dodge.*

And they can be similar to subordinating conjunctions.

> ***The day that** we crossed the river, we pushed on toward Dodge.*

We can use these to get precise times, too.

> *Ten seconds after we entered the river, the trouble started.*

Interestingly, for simultaneous action, we can use one of the nouns of time with or without a preposition and mean essentially the same thing.

> *My first **semester** at Texas State, I made excellent grades*
> ***During** my first **semester** at Texas State, I made excellent grades*

Any noun of time may be used in this way. And they may be used with the prepositions *before, of,* and *after* to show progression in time.

> ***The year before** their big fight, they lived together happily.*
> ***The year of** their big fight, they spent lots of money on lawyers.*
> ***The year after** their big fight, they went their separate ways.*

Sometimes the connective word *when* or *that* is omitted following one of these nouns of time.

The day *we crossed the river, we pushed on toward Dodge.*

Exercise 9.

1 Write two sentences connected by a noun of time functioning like a conjunctive adverb.
   Example: He caught a cold. **The next week**, *he caught the flu.*

2. Write a sentence with a prepositional phrase modifying a noun of time.
   Example: **The week after** *catching a cold, he caught the flu.*
   The day before *our test, we studied all day*

3. Write a sentence with noun of time followed by a clause introduced by *before*.
   Example: **The day before** *we left, we packed our bags.*

4. Write a sentence with noun of time followed by a clause introduced by *after*.
   Example: **The day after** *I lost my keys, I found them under my car seat.*

5. Write a sentence with noun of time followed by a clause introduced by *that*.
   Example: **The week that** *he worked overtime, he made fifty-five more dollars.*

Exercise 10.

Change these two sentences to connect them using the connective or structure listed.

1. Use a conjunctive adverb.

2. Use a prepositional phrase which function like a conjunctive adverb.

3. Use a preposition

4. Use a subordinating conjunction.

Exercise 11.
Change these two sentences to connect them using the connective or structure listed.
The boy was washing his dog. The boy was listening to the radio.

1. Use a conjunctive adverb.

2. Use a subordinating conjunction

3. Use a restrictive relative clause

4. Use a restrictive present-participle phrase

Connecting Causes With Results

Connecting by Juxtaposition

Just as we did with time, we may suggest a cause and result connection between two actions just by placing them side by side.

I walked into the classrooms. My students quit reading, closed their textbooks, and got out their notebooks.

There are no adverbials in these two sentences, but the reader knows that at the time I came in the students were reading. They then did the three actions one after the other. One might also infer that the reason they did the three actions was that I came into the room.

Exercise 1

1. Write two sentences which have actions that occur one after the other, the first of which apparently caused the second. Do not use a connective word.
Example: The child was hit by a baseball. He cried.

2. Write two sentences which have actions that occur one after the other, the first of which apparently caused the second. Use *and* to connect the two sentences.
*Example: We won the game. **And** we really celebrated.*

3. Write two independent clauses which have actions that occur one after the other, the first of which apparently caused the second. Use *and* to connect the two clauses.
*Example: I lost my keys, **and** I couldn't start my car.*

Connecting with Coordinating Conjunctions

We have two other coordinating conjunctions which will allow us to make it clear that there is a cause and result relationship between the two actions or conditions. One, *for,* is rather formal. When we use it, we place the result before the cause.

*Example: The candidate from Iowa withdrew from the presidential race, **for** he had been unable to raise sufficient funds to make him a viable candidate.*

The other coordinating conjunction of cause, *so*, is more informal and is thus used much more frequently. It has the added advantage of having the cause first then the result. Using *so* is my preferred way to show a cause and result relationship because it makes the connection without attracting much attention, allowing the emphasis to be placed on the more important cause and result.

*The candidate from Iowa had been unable to raise sufficient funds to make him a viable candidate, **so** he withdrew from the presidential race.*

*We won the game, **so** we really celebrated.*

Both of these coordinating conjunctions are preceding independent clause, so they may be used to introduce separate sentences. When they introduce sentences, no comma is placed after them unless you need a pair of commas to set off a parenthetical expression.

*We won the game. **So** we really celebrated.*

*The candidate from Iowa withdrew from the presidential race. **For** he had been unable to raise sufficient funds to make him a viable candidate.*

*After a great start, Wake Forest lost its last six games. **So**, of course, they were not invited to the NCAA tournament.*

Exercise 2

1. Write two sentences which have actions that occur one after the other, the first of which caused the second. Use *so* to connect them.
   *Example: The child was hit by a baseball. **So** he cried.*

2. Write two sentences which have actions that occur one after the other, the second of which caused the first. Use *for* to connect them.
   *Example: The oil company reported record profits. **For** the price of gasoline rose steadily during the quarter.*

3. Write two independent clauses which have actions that occur one after the other, the first of which caused the second. Use *so* to connect them.
   *Example: The child was hit by a baseball, **so** he cried.*

4. Write two independent clauses which have actions that occur one after the other, the second of which caused the first. Use *for* to connect them.
   *Example: The oil company reported record profits, **for** the price of gasoline rose steadily during the quarter.*

Connecting with Conjunctive Adverbs

Just as with time connection, we can use conjunctive adverbs to show cause and result relationships. Some of these are quite formal, and we will rarely use them.

*Bob cheated on the test. **Hence**, he was suspended from school.*

*He raise massive funds for his campaign. **Thus**, he remained a viable candidate.*

Maybe Bob's suspension merited the ponderous connective, *hence*. But the slightly formal conjunctive, *therefore*, would better fit the circumstances.

*Bob cheated on the test. **Therefore**, he was suspended from school.*

Sometimes we use entire prepositional phrases to replace the conjunctive adverb.

*Bob cheated on the test. **As a result**, he was suspended from school.*

*Bob cheated on the test. **For that reason**, he was suspended from school.*

Exercise 3

Use a conjunctive adverb or prepositional phrase of cause and result in each of the exercises below. Choose from conjunctive adverbs such as *consequently, thus, hence, or therefore* or use a prepositional phrase such as *for that reason, because of that,* or *as a result.*

1. Write two sentences which have actions that occur one after the other, the first of which caused the second. Use a conjunctive adverb to connect them.

    Example: I won the first match. ***Therefore,*** *I advanced to the semifinals.*

2. Write two sentences which have actions that occur one after the other, the first of which caused the second. Use a conjunctive adverb to connect them. Don't begin the second sentence with the conjunctive adverb.

    Examples: I won the first match. I, ***therefore,*** *advanced to the semifinals.*
    I won the first match. I advanced to the semifinals, ***therefore.***

3. Write two sentences which have actions that occur one after the other, the first of which caused the second. Use a prepositional phrase to connect them.

    Example: I won the first match. ***As a result,*** *I advanced to the semifinals.*

4. Write two sentences which have actions that occur one after the other, the first of which caused the second. Use a conjunctive adverb to connect them. Don't begin the second sentence with the conjunctive adverb.

    Example: The candidate from Iowa had been unable to raise sufficient funds to make him a viable candidate. He, ***for that reason,*** *withdrew from the presidential race.*

Connecting with Prepositions

The result clause or sentence can be converted into a present participle or a noun and become the object of a preposition.

Because of *my victory in the first match, I advanced to the semifinals.*

The oil company reported record profits ***as a result of*** *the steady rise in the price of gasoline during the quarter*

As a result of *Bob's cheating on the test, he was suspended from school.*

Owing to and *due to* are prepositions of cause which are usually not used in academic writing but are common in informal prose.

Exercise 4

Use a preposition of cause in each of the exercises below. Choose from prepositions such as *because of, for,* or *as a result of.*

1. Write a sentence with a prepositional phrase of cause. The causal phrase should appear first.
   Examples: **As a result of** *Bob's cheating on the test, he was suspended from school.*
   Because of *Bob's misbehavior, he was punished.*

2. Write a sentence with a prepositional phrase of cause. The causal phrase should appear last.
   Examples: He won **because of** *his good serve.*
   He was arrested **for** *stealing*
   He was arrested **for** *theft.*

Connecting with Subordinating Conjunctions

Instead of those effective preposition, I more commonly use the equally effective subordinating conjunction *because.*

Because *Bob cheated, he was suspended.*
Bob was suspended **because** *he cheated.*

Notice that *because of* is always a preposition and that *because* without the *of* is always a subordinating conjunction.

In informal writing, the subordinating conjunctions, since and as, are used to express a causal connection. I try to avoid using them for this in formal prose because in some context they can be ambiguous.

Since *I have been here, I have been happy.*

Does this say that I have been happy as a result of being here or not?
I also avoid wordy compound subordinating conjunctions which include the fact that: as a result of the fact that, because of the fact that, owing to the fact that, and due to the fact that. And I avoid seeing as how because it seems too informal.

Exercise 5

1. Write a sentence with *because*. The causal clause should appear first.
   Examples: **Because** *Bob misbehaved, he was punished.*

2. Write a sentence with *because*. The causal clause should appear last.
   Example: He won the tennis match **because** *he served well.*

3. Write a sentence with *because*. The causal clause should appear in the middle.
   Example: Bill Simpson, **because** *he was rich, retired early.*

Connecting with Present Participles

Still another way to show a causal connection is by using the nonrestrictive adjectivals which we studied in previous lessons. The most common of these are those of thinking and knowing followed by a nominal clause introduced by *that*.

> ***Knowing*** *that he was late, Bill called Marsha to explain.*
> *Bill,* ***believing*** *that Marsha would be angry, decided to skip Marsha's party.*

These mean essentially the same as the following sentences with subordinating conjunctions of cause.

> ***Because*** *he knew that he was late, Bill called Marsha to explain.*
> *Bill,* ***because*** *he believed that Marsha would be angry, decided to skip her party.*

Exercise 6.

1 Write a sentence with a present-participle phrase of thinking after the noun it modifies.
   Example: Andrea, ***figuring*** *that I would be late, left the food in the oven.*

2. Write a sentence with a present-participle phrase of thinking front-shifted.

Example: **Supposing** *that there would be no hot food at home, I bought a Jumbo Jack.*

Connecting with Adjective Phrases

Similarly, we can get used certain nonrestrictive adjective phrases to show cause.

> **Sure** *that he had a promotion, Bill bought a new car.*
> **Fearful** *of another attack, the soldier dug deeper trenches.*
> *Susan,* **confident** *that she had made the shot, threw her fist into the air.*

The same sentence I used to illustrate time in the last lesson can show a causal connection, too. As well as front-shifted. the adjective phrase can come after the subject.

> *Jim,* **angry** *about not knowing where his children were even though it was past midnight and on a cold stormy night, called his wife at work.*

And the adjective phrase may come last.

> *I went to the party,* **certain** *that I would be welcomed heartily.*

Exercise 7.

1   Write a sentence with an adjective phrase after the noun it modifies.
Example: Tom Smith, **proud** *of his writing skill, showed Minerva his essay.*

2. Write a sentence with an adjective phrase front-shifted before the subject.
> *Example:* **Sure** *that the punctuation was correct, Tom Smith turned in the essay.*

3. Write a sentence with an adjective phrase end-shifted.
> *Example: I didn't go to the party,* **unsure** *of my welcome.*

Connecting with Nouns of Cause

One common way to show a connection between two actions or conditions is to use a noun of cause: *cause, effect, reason, result.*

*The **cause** for our loss was our poor shooting.*
*The **reason** for our loss was our poor shooting.*
*The **result** of our poor shooting was that we lost.*
*The **effect** of our poor shooting was that we lost.*

These are not my preferred way to show cause and result. I much prefer one of these three.

Because we shot poorly, we lost.
We shot poorly, so we lost.
Because of our poor shooting, we lost.

These convey the same information more succinctly and emphatically.

Connecting with Verbs of Cause

I usually prefer to avoid verbs of cause, also.

*Our poor shooting **caused** us to lose.*
*Our poor shooting **resulted** in us losing.*
*His tardiness **made** Marsha angry.*
*His promotion **led** to his purchase of the car.*
*Bob **made** me repair his car.*
*Bob **forced** me to repair his car.*

There are verbs that have the causal idea in the suffix. They end in –ize,-ify or -ate.

He will purify the water.
He will sanitize the bath room
They satiated the masses.

Connecting with Pronouns

I avoid employing pronouns to make the causal connections because often their reference is unclear.

We shot poorly, which was why we lost.
We shot poorly. This was why we lost.

Redundant Statement of cause

Avoid doubling up on causal words. There is one common redundancy:

*The **reason** why we lost was **because** of our poor shooting.*

This is easy to correct.

*We lost **because** of our poor shooting.*

Connecting to Show Motive

One special type of causal connection is that of motive. We also employ prepositions and subordinating conjunctions to show motive.

*I went to the store **for** milk.*
*I went to the store **so that** I could buy milk.*
*I went to the store **so** I could buy milk.*
*My wife saved money **in order that** we might take a trip.*

We may use an infinitive phrase instead of these.

*I went to the store **in order to buy** milk.*
*I went to the store **to buy** milk.*
*My wife saved money **for us to take** a trip.*
*My wife saved money **in order for us to take** a trip.*

These infinitives of motive may always have the structure words *in order* before them. If only my wife were taking the trip, the structure word *for* and the subject of the infinitive would be redundant.

*My wife saved money **for her** to take a trip.*

Instead, I would write.

My wife saved money to take a trip.

One other way to show motive is by using the nouns *motive* and *purpose*.

*My **purpose** in going to the store was to buy milk.*
*Her **motive** for saving money was to take a vacation.*

Exercise 8.

1   Write a sentence with a prepositional phrase showing motive.
Example: Bob works on the internship for the experience.

2. Write a sentence with a subordinating conjunction introducing the clause of motive.
Example: Bob works on the internship so that he will gain experience.

3. Write a sentence with an infinitive phrase of motive.
   Example: Bob works on the internship in order to gain experience.

4. Write a sentence with an infinitive phrase of motive front-shifted.
   Example: In order to gain experience, Bob works on the internship.

5. Write a sentence with an infinitive phrase of motive. The subject of the infinitive phrase must be different from that of the main clause.
   Example: In order for the team to be successful, the coach insisted that every player must practice hard.

Connecting with Complementary Clauses

Adjectives of emotion often have complementary *that* clauses, *about* prepositional phrase, and infinitive phrase which explain the cause of the emotion.

> *He is happy **that** he won the race.*
> *He is happy **about** winning the race.*
> *He is happy to have won the race.*

These mean essentially the same thing as "Because he won the race, he is happy."

Exercise 9.

1 Write a sentence with an *about* prepositional phrase complementing an adjective of emotion such as *sad, sorry, ashamed, happy, glad.*
   *Example: Bob was sad **about** the death of his grandfather.*

2 Write a sentence with a *that* clause complementing an adjective of emotion.
   *Example: Bob was sad **that** his grandfather died.*

3 Write a sentence with an *infinitive* phrase complementing an adjective of emotion.
   Example: Bob was glad to be home again.

Connecting with Intensifying Clause Complements

Adjectives and adverbs are often complemented by *so* and a *that* clause which express some intensity.

> *He was **so** tired **that** he slept for ten hours.*
> *He ran **so** fast **that** he escaped his pursuers.*

These imply that the intensity of the adjective and adverb caused the action of the *that* clause.

> *Because he was very tired, he slept for ten hours.*
> *Because he ran very fast, he escaped his pursuers.*

If we wish to complement an adjective of emotion, we can write a sentence where we have both of the last two structures.

> *He was so angry about missing the shot that he kicked the basketball.*

So we have a series of causes and results. His missing the shot caused his anger. And the anger resulted in his kicking the ball.

Exercise 10.

1 Write a sentence with an intensifying clause complementing an adjective.
Example: Bob was so smart that he made good grades without studying much.

2 Write a sentence with an intensifying clause complementing an adverb.
Example: Bob worked so carefully that he rarely made a mistake.

3 Write a sentence with an *infinitive* phrase complementing an adjective of emotion such as *sad, sorry, ashamed, happy, or glad* and with an intensifying clause.
Example: Bob was so glad to be home again that he gave a party for all his old friends.

Exercise 11.

Take the following two sentences and change them according to the directions. Be sure to punctuate them properly according to the earlier examples in this lesson.

Bob lost in the semifinals. Bob was eliminated

1. Write one sentence using *for*, a coordinating conjunction of cause.

    Example: Bob was eliminated, for he lost in the semifinals.

2. Write one sentence using *so*, a coordinating conjunction of cause.

3. Write one sentence using a subordinating conjunction of cause.

4. Write one sentence using a preposition of cause.

5. Write two sentence using a conjunctive adverb of cause.

6. Write one sentence using a noun of cause.

7. Write one sentence using a verb of cause.

Lesson 10

Connecting For Contrast

We often observe how one thing is different from something else and wish to report our observation to our reader. We also have certain expectations of how things work and are surprised when things do not work out as we expect. We often report on our surprise and report what replaced the thing we expected. To make these reports to our readers, we have available to us several different grammatical structures.

Connecting by Juxtaposition

Just as we did with time and cause, we may suggest a difference, a surprise, or replacement just by placing items side by side.

Bill plays basketball. George plays baseball.

There are no adverbials in these two sentences, but the reader knows that the two boys are playing different sports. To report my surprise, I can also get by without a connective word.

I thought I would like majoring in accounting. I didn't.

And to show replacement, I can also get by without a connective word.

I thought I would get a bike for Christmas. I got a car.

Exercise 1

1. Write two sentences which report a difference between two items. Do not use a connective word.
   Example: Bill weighs three hundred pounds. His wife weighs one hundred.

2. Write two sentences which report a surprise. Do not use a connective word.
   Example: I rushed to the store. It was closed.

3. Write two sentences which report a replacement. Do not use a connective word.
   Example: I wanted to be an hour early. I was an hour late.

Connecting with Coordinating Conjunctions

The connective word *and* can be used to imply contrast.

> *Bill weighs three hundred pounds,* **and** *his wife weighs one hundred.*
> *I rushed to the store,* **and** *it was closed.*
> *I wanted to be an hour early,* **and** *I was an hour late.*

But more often, we want to be sure the reader knows about the contrast we have observed, so we employ the effective and muted coordinating conjunctions *but* and *yet*.

> *Bill weighs three hundred pounds,* **but** *his wife weighs one hundred.*
> *I rushed to the store,* **but** *it was closed.*
> *I wanted to be an hour early,* **but** *I was an hour late.*

These coordinating conjunctions are preceding independent clauses, so they may be used to introduce separate sentences. When they introduce sentences, no comma is placed after them unless we need a pair of commas to set off a parenthetical expression.

> *Bill weighs three hundred pounds.* **But** *his wife weighs one hundred.*
> *I rushed to the store.* **But** *it was closed.*
> *I wanted to be an hour early.* **But***, as usual, I was an hour late.*

Exercise 2

1. Write two clauses which report a difference between two items. Use one of the coordinating conjunctions *but* or *yet*.
   Example: Bill is tall, **but** *his brother is short.*

2. Write two clauses which report a surprise. Use one of the coordinating conjunctions *but* or *yet*.
   Example: I was out of work for two months, **yet** *we managed to scrape by.*

3. Write two clauses which report a replacement. Use one of the coordinating conjunctions *but* or *yet*.
   Example: I ordered mustard on my Jumbo Jack, **yet** *I got mayonnaise and ketchup.*

4. Write two sentences which report a difference between two items. Use one of the coordinating conjunctions *but* or *yet*.
   *Example: Bill is large. **Yet** he isn't strong.*

5. Write two sentences which report a surprise. Use one of the coordinating conjunctions *but* or *yet*.
   *Example: I studied the material. **Yet** I never understood it.*

6. Write two sentences which report a replacement. Use one of the coordinating conjunctions *but* or *yet*.
   *Example: They were searching for oil. **But** they discovered natural gas.*

Connecting with Conjunctive Adverbs

Just as with time and cause connections, we can use conjunctive adverbs to show contrast. Some of these connectives are quite formal, and we will rarely use them.

*Bob cheated on the test. **Nonetheless**, he was not suspended from school. He raise massive funds for his campaign. **Nevertheless**, he was never a viable candidate.*

I prefer and often use the relatively informal conjunctive adverb *however*.

*Bob cheated on the test. **However**, he was not suspended from school.*

And I can use equally informal *though*, but I must place it at the end of the second clause.

*Bob cheated on the test. He was not suspended from school, **though**.*

Sometimes we use entire prepositional phrases to replace the conjunctive adverb.

*Bob wastes his money. **In contrast**, his wife is exceptionally frugal. Tim won the semifinal match easily. **On the other hand**, he played miserably in the finals.*

When we wish to show a replacement, we use the conjunctive adverb *instead*.

*I ordered mustard on my Jumbo Jack. **Instead,** I got mayonnaise and ketchup.*

My students sometimes use both *but* and *instead* in sentences such as the one above. The *but* is unnecessary since *instead* does the job nicely without the redundancy.

Exercise 3

1. Write two sentences which report a difference between two items. Use the conjunctive adverb *however.*
   *Example: Bill is large. **However,** he isn't strong.*

2. Write two sentences which report a surprise. Use the conjunctive adverb *however.*
   *Example: I studied the material. **However,** I never understood it.*

3. Write two sentences which report a replacement. Use the conjunctive adverb *instead.*
   *Example: They were searching for oil. **Instead,** they discovered natural gas.*

4. Write two sentences which report a difference between two items. Use the conjunctive adverb *however,* but do not start the second sentence with it.
   *Examples: Bill is large. He, **however,** isn't strong.*
   *Bill is large. He isn't strong, **however.***

5. Write two sentences which report a surprise. Use the conjunctive adverb *though* at the end of the second sentence
   *Example: I studied the material. I never understood it, **though.***

6. Write two sentences which report a difference between two items. In the second use the prepositional phrase *in contrast* or *on the other hand.*
   *Examples: Bill has no money. Tom, **on the other hand,** is rich.*
   *Tom is healthy. **In contrast,** Bill is sickly.*

Connecting with Prepositions

To show difference or surprise, we may use the prepositions *in spite of*, *in contrast to*, and *despite*.

> **In spite of** *cheating on the test, Bill was not suspended from school.*
> **Despite** *raising massive funds for his campaign, he was never a viable candidate.*
> **In contrast to** *his wife's frugality, Bill was a wastrel.*

To show a replacement, we use the preposition *instead of*, *in place of*, or *in lieu of*.

> **Instead of** *the mustard that I ordered, I got mayonnaise and ketchup on my Jumbo Jack.*

Exercise 4

1. Write a sentence which reports a difference or surprise between two things. Use the preposition *despite* or *in spite of*.
   Examples: **In spite of** *his large size, Bill isn't strong.*
   Bill isn't strong **despite** *being large.*

2. Write a sentence which reports a replacement. Use the preposition *instead of*, *in place of*, or *in lieu of*.
   Example: **Instead of** *paying the rent, Bill bought lottery tickets.*

Connecting with Subordinating Conjunctions

Instead of those effective preposition, I commonly use the equally effective subordinating conjunctions *although* and *even though*.

> **Although** *Bob cheated, he was not suspended.*
> *Bob wasn't suspended* **even though** *he cheated.*

The subordinating conjunction *although* is sometimes shortened to *though*. Be careful not to confuse this shortened form with the conjunctive adverb with the same spelling.

> **Bob** *was not suspended* **though** *he cheated.*
> *Bob cheated. He was not suspended,* **though**.

In the first sentence *though* is the short form of the subordinating conjunction *although*. In the second the conjunctive adverb *though* is set off by a comma and a period.

Avoid wordy compound subordinating conjunctions which include *the fact that*: *despite the fact that, in spite of the fact that,* and *in contrast to the fact that.*

> ***In spite of the fact that*** *Bob misbehaved, he was not punished.*

Exercise 5

1. Write a sentence with *although* beginning the sentence.
Examples: ***Although*** *Bob misbehaved, he was not punished.*

2. Write a sentence with *although*'s shortened form *though.* Do not begin the sentence with it.
*Example: He won the tennis match **though** he served poorly.*

Connecting with Nouns of Contrast

A less successful way of conveying difference, surprise, and replacement is by using a noun.

> *I recognized the **difference** in size between Bob and Tom.*
> *It was quite a **surprise** to everybody when Bill was not suspended for cheating.*
> *The **replacement** of mustard with mayonnaise displeased me.*

These are not my preferred way to show these connections.

Connecting with Verbs of Contrast

I usually prefer to avoid verbs of contrast, also.

> *Bob **differs** from Tim in his wasteful spending.*
> *Bob's wasteful spending **contrasts** with his wife's thrift.*
> *They **replaced** my mustard with mayonnaise.*
> *I was **surprised** that Bill was not suspended for cheating.*

Connecting with Adjectives

I don't use the adjective *different* much either.

*Bill is **different** from George in size.*

Connecting with Comparative Clauses

Much more useful is the comparative clause of contrast.

*Bill is larg**er than** Fred.*
*Bill is **less** intelligent **than** Jim.*
*Bill eats **more** quickly **than** Helen.*
*Bill is not **so** careful with money **as** his wife is.*

Lesson 11

Making Other Logical Connections

Connecting to Show Conditions

There are no coordinating conjunctions of condition, but most of the kinds of connectives we saw with contrast are available to us to show conditional connections.

Using a Conjunctive Adverb

I know of only one conjunctive adverb to show condition, *otherwise*.

I must finish my theme tonight. **Otherwise**, *I will get points taken off.*

We can use prepositional phrases which work in much the same manner as conjunctive adverbs.

It may rain. **In that case,** *we won't play the game today.*
We may lose in the semifinals today. **In that event,** *we will leave tomorrow.*

Using Prepositions

There are a couple of common compound prepositions which are used to show a conditional connection *in case of* and *in the event of*.

In case of *a rainout, we will play tomorrow.*
In the event of *a poor showing by the starting pitcher, the manager has his ace reliever ready to go.*

Using Subordinating Conjunctions

This most common way to show a conditional connection is by using the subordinating conjunction *if*. But there are several other subordinating conjunctions of condition: *providing that, provided that, unless, in the event that*, and *in case that*.

If *it rains, we won't play.*
Unless *our fifth player shows up, we will have to forfeit.*
Provided that *I have enough money, I am going to the World Series this year.*
Providing that *he does the work well, we will give him a raise.*
In case that *I get the job, I will have to move away.*
In the event that *we finish first, we will get a trophy.*

In the last four sentence, we could shorten the connectives by leaving out the *that*s, and the sentences would still be clear. But I still prefer the shorter *if* and *unless* to show the conditional connection.

Exercise 1

1. Write a sentence with *if* beginning the sentence.
   *Example: **If** Bob misbehaved, he should be punished.*

2. Write a sentence with *unless* not at the beginning.
   *Example: He will be eligible **unless** he fails math.*

3. Write two sentences with *otherwise* at the beginning of the second sentence.
   *Example: I must pass math. **Otherwise**, I will be ineligible.*

4. Write two sentences with *in that case* at the beginning of the second sentence.
   *Example: He will probably fail math. **In that case**, he will be ineligible.*

5. Write a sentence with *in case of* at the beginning.
   *Example: **In case of** a failure in math, I will be ineligible.*

Connecting for Addition

The most common way to show addition is of course the coordinating conjunction *and*. And it works so well, we hardly need any other way, but we do have some.

Using Conjunctive Adverbs

There are several effective conjunctive adverbs. I prefer the informal and inobtrusive ones, *too* and *also*. Sometimes these are so muted that we do not set them off with commas. But there also some more formal ones: *moreover, what's more, plus, additionally,* and *besides*.

*He won the Open for the seventh consecutive year. **Moreover**, he won without making a single bogey.*

Of the prepositional phrases which function similarly to these conjunctive adverbs, the most often used is *in addition*.

> *He scored thirty-three points.* **In addition***, he handed out twelve assists.*

Using Prepositions

The most often used preposition of addition is *with*, followed by *in addition to* and *along with*.

> **With** *his wife's help, Tim can stay sober.*
> **In addition to** *scoring thirty-three points, Bob handed out eleven assists.*
> **Along with** *working in the mines, he played guitar for a blues band.*

Using Subordinating Conjunctions

English has no subordinating conjunctions of addition that I would recommend. They are all the *the fact that* composites: *in addition to the fact that, with the fact that, along with the fact that, plus the fact that*

Exercise 2

1. Write a sentence with *in addition to* at the beginning of the sentence.
   Example: **In addition to** *acting, Forrest Whitaker can sing.*

2. Write two sentence with *in addition* at the beginning of the second.
   Example: Bill can play the harmonica. **In addition***, he can sing.*

3. Write two sentences with *moreover* at the beginning of the second sentence.
   Example: He is a hard worker. **Moreover***, he will work for next to nothing.*

4. Write two sentences with *also* at the beginning of the second sentence.
   Example: The quarterback completed thirty passes. **Also***, he was never sacked.*

5. Write two sentence with *too* at the end of the second.
   *Example: Bob teaches Maria math. He instructs her in English, **too**.*

Connecting For Location

There are no coordinating conjunctions of location. The preposition is the dominant structure word to connect things by location.

Using Conjunctive Adverbs

We do use conjunctive adverbs of location rather frequently to convey change of context. Some of the common connectives are *inside, outside, upstairs, downstairs, nearby, farther away.*

> *The farmers were cutting his hay. **Nearby**, his wife was canning her fall vegetables.*
> *Bill was talking to Sally. **Not far away**, her fiancé was watching them carefully.*
> *The cowboys were in town. Back at the ranch, the rustlers were at work.*

Prepositional phrases serve the same function by showing the change of context information.

> *The cowboys were in town. **At the ranch**, the rustlers were at work.*
> *Bill was talking to Sally. **Across the room**, her fiancé was watching them carefully.*

Using Prepositions

There are many locational functions of prepositional phrases. One of the most common is providing information about range, using *from* and *to.*

> ***From** New England **to** East Texas, the pine woods grow providing soft wood for paper and building materials.*

Most prepositions serve to connect things by their location: *up, under, down, around, above, on, into, in, in back of, in front of,* and so forth.

> ***In** English, he is a superior student, **in** math only average.*

Connecting with Subordinating Conjunctions

There are two subordinating conjunctions which connect clauses of place with main clauses: *where* and *wherever.*

*I work **where** my brother works.*
*I work **wherever** I can find a place for my tools.*

Exercise 3

1. Write a sentence using *from* and *to* to show a range.
   *Example: The first week we went **from** Austin **to** Boston.*

2. Write a sentence with *where* at the beginning.
   *Example: **Where** I worked, I had to wear a mask because of the dangerous fumes.*

3. Write a sentence with *where* not at the beginning.
   *Example: Because of the dangerous fumes, I had to wear a mask **where** I worked.*

4. Write two sentences with a conjunctive adverb of place at the beginning of the second sentence.
   *Example: We worked in the sun. **Inside**, the bosses had AC.*

5. Write two sentences with a prepositional phrase at the beginning of the second sentence.
   *Example: We were staying with Margie. **Across town**, Bill and Helen found a hotel.*

Connecting to Show Alternatives

The coordinating conjunction *or* is the most common way of showing choices.

*Bob will pitch **or** play shortstop.*
*If we expect to win, Bob has to pitch well, **or** we have to hit better than we have been.*

The conjunctive adverb *alternatively* can also connect choices.

*In order to take a vacation, Susan needs to save more money. **Alternatively**, Bob needs to spend less.*

Connecting to Show Manner

The manner in which we do an action answers the question *how*.

Using Prepositions

One common way of connecting information about manner to the main clause is by using the preposition *like*.

*That rookie plays shortstop **like** a veteran.*

The preposition of addition *with* is also frequently used to answer the question about how something is done.

*He handles the weapon **with** care.*

We have compound prepositions of manner: *in the manner of, in the fashion of, in the way of, à la.*

*Bob sculpts in the **manner** of his mentor.*
*Tim dresses in the **fashion** of the left bank.*
*He paints **à la** Mattisse.*

Another common preposition to show manner is **by**.

*He succeeding in winning the first set **by** serving well.*

Using Manner Adverbs

Using adverbs ending with –ly is our most frequent way of showing manner.

*He handles the weapon careful**ly**.*

Using Subordinating Conjunctions

Another effective way to show manner is by using the subordinating conjunctions *as, as if* and *as though*.

*The rookie works **as** a veteran does.*
*He plays **as if** he were a veteran.*

Using Present Participles

Also common is the use of a present participle to show how an action is done.

He removed the splinter, **holding** *the tweezers steady and* **watching** *through a magnifying glass.*

Using Absolute Constructions

In addition to showing a time connection, nominative absolutes can show how something is done.

He removed the splinter from his right hand, the **tweezers** *in his left.*

Using a Noun

The word *way* is often used to head a phrase which shows the manner in which an action is done.

He works the way his mentor did.

The various nouns of manner—*way, means, fashion, manner*—often are used with modification as subjects and objects of sentence, too.

I like the careful **way** *he works.*
His careful **manner** *of working is usually successful.*
Insulting his guests was the typical **way** *for Rodney Dangerfield to work.*

Using Several Connectives

We can use these various ways of showing manner in many different combinations.

He works the **way** *his mentor did, enthusiastical***ly***, his* **goal** *clearly in mind,* **as if** *his very life depended on his success.*

He lived quietly as his teacher had, seldom going out, hermitlike.

Exercise 4

1. Write a sentence using *like* to show manner.
   Example: **Like** *Hemingway, I write with short sentences.*

2. Write a sentence with *as* at the beginning.
   Example: **As** *Flaubert did, I seek* le mot juste.

3. Write a sentence with *as* not at the beginning.
   *Example: She took care of the poor in Central Texas **as** Mother Teresa did in India.*

4. Write a sentence with *both an –ly* adverb and a present-participle phrase.
   *Example: She wrote wild**ly**, rush**ing** to put her emotions into words.*

5. Write a sentence with a *with* prepositional phrase and an absolute construction.
   *Example: She rode **with** care, her **hands** holding onto the saddle horn.*

6. Write a sentence with an –ly adverb and a phrase headed by the noun *way*.
   *Example: She rode skillful**ly**, the **way** she had learned from her mother.*

7. Write a sentence with an –ly adverb and a present-participle phrase which has an *as* clause.
   *Example: She completed the assignment **hurriedly**, not proofread**ing** as her teacher had required.*

Disconnection

Lesson 12

Disconnecting From the Agent

When we write successfully, we are careful to keep our readers informed about the agent who does the various actions we describe. We make important distinctions about the interests, qualifications, age, sex, nationality, relationships, vocation of these agents. At other times we are less careful and mistakenly assume that the reader will know all of this, will know what we know. We fail to connect the agent to the action they did. There are several grammatical constructions we can fall into the habit of using which will result in our not providing the reader information he needs. Some of these structures are not bad. They serve useful purposes, but if we use them carelessly, our readers will be less well informed and perhaps confused. They also may prevent us from considering specific information about differences.

Eating snails is disgusting.

In this sentence the writer has used the present-participle phrase *eating snails* as the subject. She has not told the reader who is eating or whose opinion it is that the action is disgusting. Who is eating may be unimportant here, but who is disgusted is quite important. The sentence implies that everyone is disgusted by this action, but the writer probably meant to say only that it disgusted her.

There are several structures sometimes used by writers which should be avoided. Some have been universally condemned by teachers and have standard names, but others, just as confusing to the reader, have no standard names by which they can be condemned.

Passive Voice

Earlier we talked about passive voice, and we came to realize how valuable it could be when used properly and how confusing when used improperly. When we use passive voice, we can easily omit the agent simply by leaving off the prepositional phrase made up of *by* and the agent. For example, we can make

Fred has misplaced the tools.

passive by converting it into

The tools have been misplaced by Fred.

And we can also exercise our option of deleting the *by* prepositional phrase and get

The tools have been misplaced.

If we write this without considering the active-voice option and without considering our readers' desire to know about who is doing things, we may have made our reader unhappy unnecessarily. Perhaps we had the information and simply overlooked the need for it by making a hasty choice of the passive construction. The passive voice also can be used in combination with other agent-deleting constructions and give us difficulty as I will demonstrate in some of the examples to follow. Some students habitually use the passive without consideration of its dangers and construct sentence after sentence with no agents. Sometimes, a student may have specific people in mind who do the actions they mention, but she fails to include the information needed. Other times, a student may not have thought carefully enough about her subject. She may be thinking that it doesn't matter who does the action, that what is true for one is true for all, that there is a kind of generic human who is doing these things, an anyone. But that may not be true. Let us consider some other passive voice sentences.

The raises were denied for another year.
The reports must be given by the fifth of December without fail, or students will be punished.

Neither of these sentences may be a bad sentence in context. But if the reader needs to know who denied the raises, who must give the report, and who will punish the students and we don't tell him, then we have missed our audience, missed an opportunity to inform. Readers too often frustrated often cease to be readers, and we will have no audience.

Present-participle Phrases

When we write present-participle phrases as subjects, we often leave off the agent. We say

Throwing the trash on the roadway caused a wreck.

assuming, probably correctly, that our statement is true no matter who throws the trash. But we may have a particular person in mind. In this case, we may write

Tim's throwing the trash on the roadway caused a wreck.

We could use this sentence, or we might replace it with the more typical

Tim caused the wreck by throwing trash on the roadway.

Here are some examples of present-participles without agents,

The rules concerned not running in the halls.
Running laps may be unhealthy.
He was talking about avoiding injuries by evaluating fitness before starting out.

These could be revised in several ways

The schools rules did not allow students to run in the halls.
Running laps may be unhealthy for people out of condition.
The doctor was talking about his patients' avoiding injuries by having their fitness checked before they started out.

Infinitive Phrases

With infinitives we can also omit the agent if we wish. Instead of writing

It is difficult to understand my Spanish teacher.

it would probably be better to say.

It is difficult for me to understand my Spanish teacher.

because other people may understand Spanish better than I do. Here are some other examples of infinitives without their agents.

The idea was to enter the vault without being seen.
To win at tennis is not difficult if errors are avoided.
To eat alone in a crowded cafeteria is discouraged when first arriving on campus.
To be happy, long walks should be taken.
To be given a new car without having done a thing to deserve it would be unexpected.

You probably noticed that infinitives are used in combination with agent-less present participles and passive voice constructions. Here are some possible ways agents can be added.

The gang leader planned to get his men into the vault without their be-ing seen by the people working in the bank.
The beginning tennis player can often win simply by avoiding errors.
Psychologists discourage new students from eating alone in a crowded cafeteria.
To be happy, some avid hikers must take long walks.
I wouldn't expect my parents to give me a car unless I had done some-thing to deserve it.

Elliptical Clauses

In certain adverbial clauses, we may delete the agent and a following *be* verb without losing any clarity. For example

Before they went to the party, Fred and Mary had been playing tennis.

can be changed to

Before going to the party, Fred and Mary had been playing tennis.

without any problem because the agent of *going* is the same as the subject of the following clause. Here are some examples of faulty ellipsis — that is deleting the subject of the dependent clause when the subject is not the same as the subject of the main clause.

Although not hungry, the food was eaten.
Once punished, we let the matter drop.
Although winning easily, happiness was not gained.
Once at the front, the performers were easy to see.

We can correct these easily by changing the subject of the main clause or by adding the agent to the clause.

Although not hungry, we ate the food.
Once our attackers were punished, we let the matter drop.
Although winning easily, we still were not happy.
Once at the front, we could easily see the performers.

Past-participle Phrases

Most people know the problems of dangling past participles, so I will give only a single example of it.

Disqualified from the race for a false start, disappointment will be real after all the running which has probably been done over the past year.

I would correct this by putting the person disqualified into the sentence as the subject of the main clause,

Disqualified from the race for a false start, Fred was disappointed because he had run so much over the past years.

Present-participle Phrases

We can correct the dangling present-participle phrase quite easily by adding the agent, changing

Watching the game, the teams were evaluated on their hustle.

to

We watched the games and evaluated the team on their hustle.

Noun Phrase of Action

You remember from the first lesson that noun phrases of actions could have an agent in a possessive form or it could be written without the agent. We can say *the discovery* or *Fred's discovery.* If we leave out the possessive agent, we can confuse our readers. For example, the reader may not know who did the evaluating in

After the evaluation, reports will be sent immediately.

We can clear up the confusion by changing it to

After my evaluation of Fred, I will send him a report immediately.

Noun Phrase of Action as Attributive Nouns

Sometimes we can have trouble with action nouns when we employ them to modify other nouns and do not provide any information about agency. For example, notice how we can embed one clause idea after another by using the following passive voice sentences. At no time do we tell our readers who is doing any of this.

The consultation will be reported soon.
The consultation report will be evaluated.
The consultation report evaluation will be presented
The consultation report evaluation presentation was approved.
The consultation report evaluation presentation approval was expected.

If we tackle the difficult job of providing information omitted from just the last of these monsters, we may need several clauses.

We expect Dr. Smith to approve Bill's presentation about our evaluation of the FDA report.

I don't particularly like this either. But it is better than the uninformative sentence it replaced.

Adjective of Thinking/Feeling

We can also write sentences which have no agents by using an adjective of thought or emotion. These are much like passive voice constructions and can be revised in a similar fashion. For example we can change,

The results were predictable.
The results were believable.
The book was understandable.
The book was unreadable.

to

The results were predictable by us.
The results were believable by us.
The book was understandable by us.
The book was unreadable by us.

or better to

We predicted the results.
We believed the results.
We understood the book.
We couldn't read the book.

There is another kind of adjective much like these but the revision is somewhat different. For example we can change

The movie was boring.
Fred was likeable.
The joy was indescribable.

to

The movie was boring to us.
Fred was likeable with us.
The joy was indescribable by me.

or better

The movie bored me
We liked Fred.
I could not describe my joy.

Adverbs of Thinking

We sometimes use adverbs similar to these thinking/feeling adjectives. In these too there is an unstated agent for these actions or judgments buried in the adverb.

Understandably, the reports will be filed late.
Predictably, she went out with Fred again after all her complaining.
Unfortunately, A &M beat Texas.
Miraculously, Fred was not punished.
Surprisingly, Marge was not invited to the party.

Who did the understanding and the predicting? Who thought it unfortunate, miraculous, and surprising? The reader can't know for sure. We can revise the sentences to make them clearer by using noun clauses or nominal infinitive phrases.

We understand that the committee will file its report late.
I would have predicted that, even after her complaints, Mary would go out with Fred again.
We Texas fans hated for A & M to beat Texas.
I thought it was a miracle that Fred was not punished.
I was surprised that Marge was not invited to the party.

Indefinite *You*

Now we must deal with the main way student writers hide the agent from the reader. They use the second person pronoun *you*. This *you* is often used to refer to just anyone, and often causes no trouble, but other times it causes trouble because the writer intends the *you* to refer not to people in general but to a small group. For example a student might write,

When you get arrested for murder at the age of sixteen, something is really wrong.

And any reader is going to know that this *you* is not him and is not people in general but is a reference to a specific person or small group of persons. Some teachers write in the margin, "Who? Me?" Other teachers become so continually incensed by this usage that they tell their students never to use *you* under any circumstances. And that is not bad advice, but students see professional writers using *you* successfully and wonder why it is wrong for them. Here are some examples illustrating the improper use of *you*.

> *You go into the woods wearing camouflage clothing.*
> *You can get thrown out of a bar if you get in a fight.*
> *When you come out of the shower in the girl's dorm, a cold blast of air hits you.*

We can easily improve these by putting in the specific agents the writer probably had in mind.

> *A safety-conscious hunter goes into the woods wearing camouflage clothing.*
> *Bar brawlers usually get thrown out.*
> *When I came out of the shower in the dorm, I was hit by a cold blast of air.*

Indefinite *One*

We can also misuse the indefinite *one*.

> *If one doesn't behave, punishment will be given.*

We can change this to

> *Miss Jones punishes the students who misbehave in her class.*

or

> *Fred misbehaved in Miss Jones' class, so she threw him out.*

depending on whether or not we had a specific instance in mind or not.

Indefinite *One* and *They*

Some students increase their error by shifting from the singular *one* to the plural *they*, *them*, or *their*. For example, they write

> *One must behave, or they will be ejected.*

We can improve this by writing.

My mother's student's must behave, or she ejects them.

or

I have to behave or be thrown out.

Indefinite *Person*

Sometimes we hide the specific person or group of people by using the all encompassing *person*. For example someone might write,

A person has to watch what he spends, or he will wish he hadn't.

The statement is true for most people, but there are many wealthy people who could never spend all their money and would never worry about it. The writer probably has a particular group in mind even though he used the general noun *person*.

I have to watch what I spend, or I will not have enough money to finish the semester.

or

Students who spend their money partying often regret it when they have no grocery money.

Indefinite *Person* and *They*

Here too students have trouble because they shift to the plural *they* after first using the singular *person*.

A person has to behave, or they will be ejected.

We can improve this in any of several ways,

My mother's students have to behave, or they are ejected.
She ejects students who misbehave.

Other Ways to Hide Agent

There are several other ways we mistakenly hide the agent. Here is an example of each. How would you revise these to provide information about agency?

Indefinite *People*

People have to behave, or they will be thrown out.

Indefinite Whoever

Whoever misbehaves will be ejected.

Indefinite *Whoever* with *Their*

Whoever eats grapefruits cares about their health.

Indefinite Pronoun

Anyone misbehaving will be ejected
Everyone likes Fred.

Indefinite Pronoun and *They*

Anyone caught driving while intoxicated will have their licenses suspended.

Exercise

Revise the following sentences to make clear who is doing what.

1. Unhappily, the work was poorly done.

2. Getting to class late is not a good idea.

3. To survive in college, hard work may not be enough.

4. While working on a roof, accidents can happen.

5. You get the bends when you come to the surface too fast.

6. The decision not to run was surprising.

7. When taking English, plagiarizing is not good.

8. Caught plagiarizing, all hell broke loose.

9. Looking deep into the water, the rocks could be seen without difficulty.

10. Having been defeated by a single point, anger was all that was there.

11. It is dangerous to ride a poorly-trained pony.

12. One can risk injury by climbing alone and by not checking their tools.

13. Going home without any money and lots of dirty clothes is a problem, but one knows that their parents will be there.

14. The discussion was about going to the coast, but no decision was made because of the lack of information about how much money you had to have to stay at some of the larger hotels or condominiums there.

Appendix 1

Answers

Lesson 1

Exercise 1

Change the sentence to a possessive agent and a noun

1.	I worked.	*Example: my work*
2.	I suggested.	*Example: my suggestion*
3.	I insisted.	*Example: my insistence*
4.	I perused.	my perusal
5.	I renewed.	my renewal
6.	I planned.	my plan
7.	I stated.	my statement
8.	I reverted.	my reversion
9.	I delayed.	my delay
10.	I persevered.	my perseverance
11.	I continued.	my continuation
12.	I destroyed.	my discovery
13.	Sally flirted.	Sally's flirtation
14.	Bill resigned.	Bill's resignation
15.	Tom distributed.	Tom's distribution
16.	Tom converted.	Tom's conversion
17.	Tom sneezed.	Tom's sneeze
18.	Carl complained.	Carl's complaint
19.	Max repeated.	Max's repetition

Exercise 2

Now reverse the procedure and change the noun phrase to a sentence.

1	my help	*I helped.*
2.	my assistance	*I assisted.*
3.	my accusation	*I accused.*
4.	my disapproval	*I disapproved.*
5.	my doubt	I doubted.
6.	my belief	I believed.
7.	my desire	I desired.
8.	my reversal	I reversed.

Exercise 4

Convert the following sentences to noun phrases by converting the adjective into a noun.

1. Mary was beautiful.	*Mary's beauty*
2. Fred was insistent.	*Fred's insistence*
3. Fred was angry.	*Fred's anger*
4. Carol was hasty.	*Carol's haste* or *hastiness.*
5. Mike was cautious.	*Mike's caution*
6. Hal was undecided.	*Hal's indecision*
7. Mike was lazy.	*Mike's laziness*
8. Sally was flirtatious.	*Sally's flirtation* or *flirtatiousness*

Exercise 6

Identify all adverbials by writing above them appropriate words from this list:

A. Point in Time
B. Frequency
C. Duration
D. Place
E. Direction.

F. Manner
G. Material
H. Means
I. Accompaniment
J. Reason/motive

Place or Direction
1. Bill went to Austin.
Place or Direction
2. Bob put the towel on the table.

manner
3. Fred plays with care

frequency time
4. Tom works every day until five.

time reason
5. I stayed here all day because of my illness.

material
6. I made the biscuits with whole-wheat flour.

time
7. I finished the lesson at five.

accompaniment
8. I did the work alone.

manner
9. He did the job a funny way.

time
10. He quit his job last semester.

manner
11. He did it out of spite.

manner
12. He works carelessly.

frequency
13. He seldom remembers mother's day.

frequency
14. Every day he goes to work drunk.

direction
15. He walked toward the beach.

material
16. He made the roof of cedar.

motive
17. He went to the store for milk.

motive
18. He worked for money.

Direction   *manner*
19. He stared at her in an angry manner.

duration
20. They fought without rest.

place   *place*
21. They stayed in the barn on the floor.

time
22. In the beginning I was happy.

manner
23. I began happily.

Lesson 3

Exercise 1

Convert the following active voice sentences to passive. Remember each must have some form of the verb *be*.

1. I finished the job.

   Example: *The job was finished by me.*

2. Tim did the work.

The work was done by Tim.

3. Tom may have destroyed the evidence.

The evidence may have been destroyed by Tom.

4. Tom struck me.

I was struck by Tom.

5. Belle Starr and Jesse James committed crimes.

Crimes were committed by Belle Starr and Jesse James.

6. Joe was eating the chips again.

The chips were again being eaten by Joe.

7. I have cut the lines.

The lines have been cut by me.

8. They sank the ship.

The ship was sunk by them.

Exercise 2

Reverse the procedure and change the following passive voice sentences into active voice sentences.

1. Baseballs were thrown into the stands by the batboy.

   Example: The batboy threw baseballs into the stands.

2. Fish are often seen by scuba divers.

Scuba divers often see fish.

3. Plankton is eaten by whales.

Whales eat plankton.

4. Carbohydrates are stored by the body.

The body stores carbohydrates.

5. Jim Smith will be rewarded for his efforts by the boss.

The Boss will reward Jim Smith for his efforts.

6. Geometry is being offered by the junior high school during the summer term.

The junior high is offering Geometry during the summer term.

7. Soon passive voice will have been taught by the teacher.

Soon the teacher will have taught passive voice.

Exercise 3

Employing the guidelines above, choose which sentence might best follow this one: "Bill Simpson had been stealing welding rods from his construction job."

2. Yesterday, he was arrested.

Exercise 4

Write an explanation of how you applied the guidelines in order to make the choice.

Bill Simpson is the old information, so *he* should go at the first of the second sentence. The *by* phrase can be left off because the policeman is the expected agent. By leaving it off, the writer can emphasize what happened to Bill.

Exercise 5

Employing the guidelines above, choose which sentence might best follow this one: "Bill complained a lot."

1. He was despised by his roommate, his boss, his teachers, his coach, his brother, even perhaps his mother.

Exercise 6

Write an explanation of how you applied the guidelines in order to make the choice.

Bill Simpson is the old information, so *he* should go at the first of the second sentence. The *by* phrase contains important new information about who the agent is, so it should not be omitted.

Exercise 7

Employing the guidelines above, choose which sentence might best follow this one: "Fred went shopping."

3. He bought beans, carrots, celery, asparagus, red peppers, and sweet onions—the new kind.

Exercise 8

Write an explanation of how you applied the guidelines in order to make the choice.

Fred is the old information, so he should go at the first of the second sentence. The active voice form should be used because the important new information in the direct object should be at the end of the second sentence.

Lesson 4

Exercise 1

Convert the dynamic kind of base sentence into a noun phrase of action.

1. He retired.	*his retirement*
2. We evaded.	our evasion
3. We discovered.	our discovery
4. She deceived.	her deception
5. She pleaded.	her plea

6. Fred apologized.	her apology
7. Bill swung wildly.	*Bill's wild swing*
8. They complained loudly.	*their loud complaints*
9. He ran for six yards.	*his six-yard run*
10. He ran a long way.	*his long run*
11. Bill smiled cunningly.	Bill's cunning smile
12. Bill burped loudly.	Bill's loud burp
13. Sara performed magnificently as Ophelia.	Sarah's magnificent performance as Ophelia.
14. Fred played in center field with enthusiasm.	Fred's enthusiastic play in center field.
15. Sam responded speedily.	Sam's speedy response
16. He fought cancer.	*his fight against* cancer
17. He discovered a cure.	*his discovery of a* cure
18. He described the house.	his description of the house
19. He avoided Roger.	His avoidance of Roger
20. Carl manipulates his friends.	Carl's manipulation of his friends

Exercise 2

Convert these to present-participle phrases.

7. Bill swung wildly.	*Bill's swinging wildly*
8. They complained loudly.	Bill's complaining loudly

9. He ran for six yards.	His running for six yards
10. He ran a long way.	His running a long way
11. Bill smiled cunningly.	Bill's smiling cunningly
12. Bill burped loudly.	Bill's burping loudly.
13. Sara performed magnificently as Ophelia.	Sara's performing magnificently as Ophelia
14. Fred played in center field with enthusiasm.	Fred's playing in center field with enthusiasm
15. Sam responded speedily.	Sam's responding speedily
16. He fought cancer.	his fighting cancer
17. He discovered a cure.	his discovering of a cure
18. He described the house.	his describing the house
19. He avoided Roger.	his avoiding Roger
20. Carl manipulates his friends.	Carl's manipulation of his friends

Exercise 3

Convert the base sentence into first an action-noun phrase and then a present-participle phrase and use each to replace *doing something*.

1. **Base:** He accused Tom.
He avoided suspicion by doing something.
    Example of Noun Phrase: *He avoided suspicion by his accusations against Tom.*
    Example of Present participle: *He avoided suspicion by accusing Tom.*

2. **Base:** He withdrew from the competition.
The match ended because of his doing something.

> Example of Noun Phrase: *The match ended because of his withdrawal from the competition.*
> Example of Present-participle Phrase: *The match ended because of his withdrawing from the competition.*

3. **Base:** He described the circumstances.
He helped the new people by doing something.

Use noun phrase: He helped the new people by his description of the circumstances
Use present-participle phrase: He helped the new people by describing the house.

4. **Base:** Bob contemplated the nature of the universe.
Bob avoided his problems by doing something.

Use noun phrase: Bob avoided his problems by contemplation of the nature of the universe
Use present-participle phrase: Bob avoided his problems by contemplating the nature of the universe

5. **Base:** He demonstrated his courage.
He inspired his men by doing something.

Use noun phrase: He inspired his men by a demonstration of his courage.
Use present-participle phrase: He helped the new people by demonstrating his courage..

6. **Base:** He assisted with the care of his grandmother.
Frederick pleased his family by doing something.

Use noun phrase: Frederick pleased his family by his assistance with the care of his grandmother.
Use present-participle phrase: He helped the new people by assisting with the care of his grandmother.

Exercise 7

Convert the prepositional phrase to an adverbial clause with a subordinating conjunction.

1. He quit in spite of liking the job.
   Example: He quit although he liked the job.

2. He lost the match because of his poor serves.

He lost the match because he served poorly.

3. He was attending college at the time of his sister's marriage.

He was attending college when his sister married.

4. He left upon the entrance of Fred.

He left when Fred entered.

5. Tim cried after the fight with Mark.

Example: Tim cried after he fought Mark.

6. He conceded defeat after losing the second set.

Example: He conceded defeat after he lost the second set.

Lesson 6

Exercise 1

Combine into one sentence using adjectival clause. **Either answer is correct**.

> *Example:* **Insert:** *The children had tickets.*
> **Matrix:** *The children entered first.*

The children who had tickets entered first.
The children that had tickets entered first.

1. **Insert**: The man lost his job.
   Matrix: The man was unhappy.

   The man who lost his job was unhappy.
   The man that lost his job was unhappy.

2. **Insert:** The trees were dying fast.
   Matrix: The trees had a strange disease.

The trees which were dying fast had a strange disease.
The trees that were dying fast had a strange disease.

3. **Insert:** The man was arrested for forgery.
   Matrix: I know the man.

   I know the man who was arrested for forgery.
   I know the man that was arrested for forgery.

4. **Insert:** The job is dangerous and hard.
   Matrix: The man got a job.

   The man got a job which is dangerous and hard.
   The man got a job that is dangerous and hard.

5. **Insert:** The river was running deep.
   Matrix: Tim and Bob crossed the river.

   Tim and Bob crossed a river which was running deep.
   Tim and Bob crossed a river that was running deep.

6. **Insert**: The man was unhappy.
   Matrix: The man lost his job.

   The man who lost his job was unhappy.
   The man that lost his job was unhappy.

7. **Insert:** The trees had a strange disease.
   Matrix: The trees were dying fast.

   The trees which had a strange disease were dying fast.
   The trees that had a strange disease were dying fast.

8. **Insert:** I know the man.
   Matrix: The man was arrested for forgery.

   A man whom I know was arrested for forgery.
   A man that I know was arrested for forgery.
   A man I know was arrested for forgery.

9. **Insert:** The man got a job.
   Matrix: The job is dangerous and hard.

The job which the man got is hard and dangerous.
The job that the man got is hard and dangerous.
The job the man got is hard and dangerous.

10. **Insert:** Tim and Bob crossed the river.
    Matrix: The river was running deep.

The river which Tim and Bob crossed was running deep.
The river that Tim and Bob crossed was running deep.
The river Tim and Bob crossed was running deep.

Exercise 2

Break into two sentences.
  Example: The people who were talking about Lisa's immorality were probably referring to Lisa on <u>As the World Turns.</u>

  Answer: The people were talking about Lisa's immorality. They were probably referring to Lisa on <u>As the World Turns.</u>

1. The man who watched the football practice when there was a scrimmage would leave if the team began to run pass patterns.

The man watched the football practice when there was a scrimmage. He would leave if the team began to run pass patterns

2. The man who talked with his buddies while he was preparing supper forgot to put baking powders in the cornbread.

The man talked with his buddies while he was preparing supper. He forgot to put baking powders in the cornbread

3. The man who wanted to be sure to watch the final NBA playoff game went to sleep quietly on the couch shortly after the tip-off.

The man wanted to be sure to watch the final NBA playoff game. He went to sleep quietly on the couch shortly after the tip-off.

Exercise 4

Convert the adjectival clause to a present-participle phrase.

*tAnswer: The man **stealing** tools from the job was fired.*

1. The pigeons that were roosting on the window air conditioner were cooing loudly and often.

The pigeons roosting on the window air conditioner were cooing loudly and often.

2. I spoke to the man who was fishing from the pier.

I spoke to the man fishing from the pier.

3. The men who were playing baseball with the children were playing without gloves.

The men playing baseball with the children were playing without gloves.

Exercise 6

Convert the adjectival clause to a past-participle phrase.

*Example: The man **who was hired** by his father was fired by his brother.*
Answer: The man **hired** by his father was fired by his brother.

1. The chickens that were raised in Arkansas were eaten in Texas.

The chickens raised in Arkansas were eaten in Texas.

2. I interviewed the man who was arrested for the crime.

I interviewed the man arrested for the crime

3. The team which was beaten by us in the first game won the tournament.

The team beaten by us in the first game won the tournament.

Lesson 7

Exercise 1

Convert the adjectival clause to either a present or past-participle phrase.

Example: Tim Todd, who was elected cheerleader for the third consecutive year, jumped about agilely on the sidelines.

Answer: Tim Todd, elected cheerleader for the third consecutive year, jumped about agilely on the sidelines.

1. Seguin High, which was beaten three consecutive weeks, fought back by trouncing Judson 35-6.

Seguin High, beaten three consecutive weeks, fought back by trouncing Judson 35-6.

2. My mother-in-law, who is wearing a magenta leotard, is taking low-impact aerobics.

My mother-in-law, wearing a magenta leotard, is taking low-impact aerobics

3. Larry Bird, who was scoring with both left and right hands, led the Celtics past the Pistons.

Larry Bird, scoring with both left and right hands, led the Celtics past the Pistons.

4. Marie-Louise, who was given an award for showmanship, has retired from teaching.

Marie-Louise, given an award for showmanship, has retired from teaching.

5. Aunt Carol, who was stealing loquats from a neighbor's tree, was caught by policemen in five squad cars.

Aunt Carol, stealing loquats from a neighbor's tree, was caught by policemen in five squad cars.

Lesson 8

Exercise 10.

Change these two sentences to connect them using the connective or structure listed. (These are not the only possible answers.)
Tim was taking a nap. His dog was barking at a cat.

1. Use a conjunctive adverb.

Tim was taking a nap. **Meanwhile**, his dog was barking at a cat.
Tim was taking a nap. **Simultaneously**, his dog was barking at a cat.

2. Use a prepositional phrase which function like a conjunctive adverb.

Tim was taking a nap. **At the same time**, his dog was barking at a cat.
Tim was taking a nap. **At that moment**, his dog was barking at a cat.

3. Use a preposition

During Tim's nap, his dog was barking at a cat.
At the time of Tim's nap, his dog was barking at a cat.

4. Use a subordinating conjunction.

While Tim was taking a nap, his dog was barking at a cat.
While his dog was barking at a cat, Tim was taking a nap.

Tim's dog was barking at a cat **while** Tim was taking a nap
Tim was taking a nap **while** his dog was barking at a cat.

Exercise 11.

Change these two sentences to connect them using the connective or structure listed. These are not the only possible answers
The boy was washing his dog. The boy was listening to the radio.

1. Use a conjunctive adverb.

The boy was washing his dog. **Meanwhile**, he was listening to the radio.
The boy was washing his dog. **Simultaneously**, he was listening to the radio.

2. Use a subordinating conjunction

While the boy was washing his dog, he was listening to the radio.
While washing his dog, the boy was listening to the radio.

3. Use a restrictive relative clause

The boy **who** was washing his dog was listening to the radio.
The boy **who** was listening to the radio was washing his dog.

4. Use a restrictive present-participle phrase

The boy wash**ing** his dog was listening to the radio.
The boy listen**ing** to the radio was washing his dog.

Appendix 2

Word List

Pronouns

Personal Pronouns

I, me, you, he, him, she, her, it, we, us, they, them

Indefinite pronoun

someone, somebody, something, anyone, anybody, anything, no one, nobody, nothing, everybody, everything, everyone, another, others

Quantitative Pronouns

some, many, much, any, more, few, less, several, all, both, each, each one, each other, neither, either, most

Demonstrative Pronouns

this, that, these, those

Possessive Pronouns

mine, yours, his, her, its, ours, theirs

Adjectivals

Demonstrative Adjectives

this, that, these, those

Possessive Adjectives

my, your, his, her, its, our, their

Verbs

Linking Verbs

be, become, remain, appear, seem, feel, get, turn, act, grow

Verbs frequently followed by Indirect Objects and Direct Objects

give, hand, throw, toss, mail, send, make, call

Verbs frequently followed by Retained Objects

be given, be handed, be thrown, be tossed, be mailed, be sent, be made, be called

Verbs frequently followed by Direct Objects and Object Complements

pick, select, elect, choose, pick, paint, name, make, call

Verbs frequently followed by Retained Object Complements

be picked, be selected, be chosen, be elected, be painted, be named, be made, be called

Verbs frequently followed by infinitive phrases with structure words *for* and *to*

hate, like, love, intend, prefer

Verbs frequently followed by infinitive phrases without structure words

want, expect, require, allow

Verbs frequently followed by indirect object and infinitive phrases

ask, tell, beg, promise, advise, order, urge, dare

Verbs frequently followed by infinitive phrases without structure words *for* and *to*

see, hear, feel, watch, listen to, smell, let, help, make, have

Verbs followed by past participle phrase as nominal

see, hear, feel, watch, listen to, smell

Auxiliary Verbs and Modals

be, have, do, may, might, can, could, shall, should, will, would, must

Compound Auxiliary Verbs

be going to, be to, be about to, be fixing to, have to, used to, ought to

Adverbials

Conjunctive Adverbs

afterwards, also, concurrently, consequently, hence, henceforth, hereafter, however, later, meantime, meanwhile, moreover, nevertheless, next, nonetheless, once, otherwise, then, thereafter, therefore, though, thus, too

Single Word Adverbs

above, accordingly, again, again and again, ahead, alone, already, also, always, annually, anyhow, anyway, anyways, anywhere, around, away, below, besides, biweekly, candidly, continually, daily, doubtless, early, endlessly, fittingly, forth, forward, frankly, frequently, honestly, however, infrequently, instead, instead, late, later, maybe, momentarily, monthly, more, never, next, now, occasionally, often, once, out, overhead, perhaps, possibly, quarterly, rarely, seldom, semiweekly, so far, sometimes, somewhere, soon, still, surely, then, together, up, weekly, yearly, yesterday, yet

Prepositional Phrases like Conjunctive Adverbs

after this, as a result, as a result of this, as a substitute, as an alternative, at this time, because of this, despite that, despite this, for a week, for that reason, from this time, in a way that accords with that, in accordance, in accordance with that, in addition, in addition to that, in conclusion, in contrast, in contrast to that, in lieu of that, in place of that, in spite of that, in summary, in summation, in that case, in that event, in time, instead of that, no doubt, of course, on occasions, on the other hand, since that time, since then, under those circumstances, within the hour

Connectives

Coordinating Conjunction

for, so, and, but, yet, or, nor

Introducers of Clause Modifying Verbs, type 1

after, although, as, because, before, if, once, provided, providing, since, so, supposing, that, though, unless, until, when, where, whereas, while

Introducers of Clause Modifying Verbs, type 1, Compounds

along with the fact that, as a result of the fact that, as often as, as if, as soon as, as soon as it happened that, as though, at the place that, at the time that, because of the fact that, despite the fact that, due to the fact that, during the time that, in addition to the fact that, in case, in case that, in contrast to the fact that, in hopes that, in order that, in spite of the fact that, owing to the fact that, plus the fact that, even though, every time that, in the event, in the event that, now that, provided that, providing that, since the time that, so that, supposing that, with the fact that, within the period of time that,

Introducers of Clause Modifying Verbs, type 2

whatever, whichever, whoever, whomever, whosoever, wherever, whenever, however, no matter what, no matter whom, no matter who, no matter which, no matter whose, no matter how, no matter when, no matter why, no matter how often, no matter how long

Introducers of Noun Clauses, type 1

no function in clause
that

Introducers of Noun Clauses, type 2

as nominals
who, whom, which, what, whose

as adjectivals
whose, which, what, how

as adverbials
how, where, when, why

Introducers of Noun Clauses, type 3

as nominals
whoever, whatever, whichever, whatever, whosoever, whatsoever

as adjectivals
whosoever, whichever, whatever, however

as adverbials
wherever, whenever, however

Introducers of Noun Clauses, type 4

no function in clause
if ___ or not, whether or not, whether___ or not

Introducers of Noun-Modifying Clauses *(Also called relative clauses and adjectival clauses)*

as nominals
who, whom, which

as adjectivals
whose

as adverbials
where, when, why

Single Word Prepositions

aboard, about, above, across, after, against, along, along with, amid, among, around, at, at, barring, before, behind, below, beneath, beside, besides, between, beyond, by, concerning, despite, down, during, except, excepting, for, from, in, inside, instead, into, like, near, of, off, on, outside, over, past, plus, regarding, respecting, save, saving only, through, throughout, till, to, together with, toward, towards, until, up, upon, with, within, without

Compound Prepositions

à la, as a result of, aside from, because of, by dint of, by means of, by the use of, by way of, contrary to, due to, for the sake of, in addition to, in advance of, in case of, in conjunction with, in consideration of, in contrast to, in hope of, in hopes of, in lieu of, in place of, in reference to, in regard to, in spite of, in the direction of, in the event of, in the fashion of, in the manner of, in the middle of, in the style of, instead of, on account of, on behalf of, out of, outside of, owing to, through the use of, with respect to, with the exception of

CPSIA information can be obtained at www.ICGtesting.com
Printed in the USA
LVOW09s1356010614

388105LV00002B/55/P